A Key to All My Houses

A Key to All My Houses

PEGGY GRAYSON

ISIS

LARGE PRINT

Oxford

First published in Great Britain 2002
by Prunus

Published in Large Print 2003 by ISIS Publishing Ltd,
7 Centremead, Osney Mead, Oxford OX2 0ES
by arrangement with the author

British Library Cataloguing in Publication Data
Grayson, Peggy
    A key to all my houses. – Large print ed. –
    (Isis reminiscence series)
    1. Grayson, Peggy – Childhood and youth
    2. Large type books
    3. England – Biography
    I. Title
    942'.083'092

ISBN 0–7531–9856–8 (hb)
ISBN 0–7531–9857–6 (pb)

Printed and bound by Antony Rowe, Chippenham

For my daughter Storm
with my love

CONTENTS

Introduction

The house in which I was born was called "Garvery", situated at the foot of a long hill leading down to the village of Hurstbourne Tarrant in Hampshire. It was, and still is (I have driven past it several times) a substantial house. At the time of my birth it had a large and rather beautiful flower garden and a croquet lawn as well as a walled vegetable and fruit garden, if the faded photographs are anything to go by. I think my parents must have run it as a private hotel as I am sure they would not have been able to afford to live there without some income.

I was christened in the village church and my father gave me a little gold chain from which was suspended a golden sovereign engraved with my name and date of birth. When I was at school this precious heirloom was pawned in one of my mother's more urgent financial crises, and never redeemed, I still mourn its loss.

We left "Garvery" when I was still a baby. To where, I am not sure, but believe it was to a flat in Bath.

These were to be the first of a long list of rented houses, rooms, flats, bungalows and cottages we lived in during my childhood. Turn the key in every door and you will find a story.

CHAPTER
ONE

Early Memories

My father was standing by the kitchen table holding aloft a large brown creature, its huge claws tied together with string. My mother took the lid off a pot of boiling water, the creature was dropped in and then with a huge leap soared up and out into the air and fell to the floor. I shrieked and on small fat legs scrambled up the stairs crying, "Babebee and dummy! Babebee and dummy!". These consisted of my general comforters, a small eiderdown and the dummy. I was all of two and a half years old!

We had gone to live in Jersey where my father had some sort of employment. I do remember boarding the small scruffy steamer that plied between England and the Channel Isles because I dropped my teddy bear over the rail when trotting up the gang plank. It fell into a sort of gully and I created hell at the top of my voice causing some intrepid sailor no doubt to risk life and limb to recover the beloved toy.

The first of my houses that I can recall was small and narrow, sandwiched in the middle of a terrace of other little houses all of the same proportions.

My mother was a great walker and nature lover and I have memories of toddling, when not being propelled in a wooden push chair, around the island, being told the names of all the flowers, grasses and trees and wondering at the cabbages growing on tall stems which I later learned were turned into walking sticks once the vegetable was harvested.

I also remember the huge piles of tomatoes, wrong shaped or sized which were turned into manure for the next year's crop. Hazy memories of a wood full of bluebells, and my father, a dedicated sea fisherman, bringing home the catch fresh and salty which my mother cooked and we ate with relish. However, it is the lobster and his reluctance to be cooked that remain the strongest memory of the house in Jersey.

From there we returned to England and lived in a bungalow in the village of Almondsbury outside Bristol. This was not far from a farm owned by my father's uncle, and we often visited him and his daughter, and these visits, which were a delight to me, continued after we left the district. I suspect that our bungalow was demolished when the motorway interchange was built, but as I have no memories of it, other than that it was rather sprawling and ugly and we were only there for a short time, that does not worry me.

I must have been three and a bit when we moved to Ireland, to a terraced house on the coast some way out of Cork, the Troubles were then at their height.

My father was already in Ireland and Mother and I had a fearful crossing in a tremendous storm, and the ship was held up for hours tossing and turning outside Cork before it could dock.

My mother was a dreadfully bad sailor and to be shut in the cabin with her all through the voyage is an abiding memory and made me vow never to go on the sea again. A vow I kept and did not venture overseas until air travel became general.

Daddy met us on the quay at Cork carrying a huge teddy bear with a lump on his back, who growled when bent forward. I was more pleased to see Daddy than the bear, as the teddy I had been given when I was born was my constant companion. However, I thanked him nicely, but this bear never achieved the favour of my first love.

The furnished house my parents rented was a grim grey edifice in a terrace of similar forbidding properties, just back from the promenade and the sea roared and thundered against the bulwark of the defences.

My mother tried planting rose bushes in the scrappy front garden, but the donkeys roaming loose knocked down the old wooden fence and demolished them all. Later, a wild storm sent the huge waves crashing over the sea wall where they rolled over the road and into our little patch and Mother gave up the unequal struggle.

The rooms in the house were high and gloomy and the furnishing shabby and uncomfortable. One day a lady came to visit my mother and take tea. I was standing leaning against Mother's side when a great wish to spend a penny overcame me. I tried to whisper to her, but she said, "Hush". I tried again with the same result. Children in those days did not interrupt the adults' conversation. So I stood there with the tears trickling down my face and warm water running down my legs before anyone noticed my plight!

My mother employed a local woman as a general maid, her name was Kathleen and she was very religious. Every time something traumatic happened she would fall on her knees, clasp her hands together and cry "Holy Mary, Mother of God, defend us". I was tremendously impressed at these performances although my mother told me to take no notice as it was only Kathleen's way of doing things.

There were shootings and trouble all around. One night the local grocer answering a knock on his door was shot dead, causing Kathleen, who was a friend of his as well as a customer, to spend longer imploring for Divine help. Once a Guards regiment came to Cork and the band in full regimentals was to parade through the streets and Kathleen took a bus to town to watch and came back, eyes like saucers.

"What did you see Kathleen?" my mother asked her.

"Ooo, M'mm" she was breathless with excitement, "they was all blowin' and beatin' and some wuz tall and some wuz short, and some wuz fat and some wuz thin, and they all wore furry hats!". My mother recounted this story over many years, which is how I remember it.

I loved Kathleen, who was kind and always had time for a small girl, and Kathleen was devoted to us. My mother, who I am sure had many anxieties, regarded her as a friend as well as an employee.

When it was fine my mother would take me for a walk along the promenade, at the end of which was a kiosk where a very old woman swathed in shawls sold home made humbugs of enormous size for a penny each. These were striped in various colours and I found them quite delicious.

My father was away a good deal, I think he had some sort of job selling things, and he returned with all sorts of stories.

His best tale was all about being invited to, and attending, a Wake. He was not quite sure what this entailed, but soon found out when he arrived at the house to see the dear departed, dressed in his best and lying in his coffin which was propped up in a corner! He said it was one of the best parties he had ever attended once you got over the initial shock. A gregarious man of great charm my father was taken to the hearts of the hospitable people of the Emerald Isle wherever he went.

We had a car, a Tin Lizzie, and at weekends Daddy would take us for drives into the very beautiful countryside. As the car was a two seater, I travelled in the "dickey", bundled in rugs to keep out the cold, and clutching hold of the picnic basket. These outings were not without their hazards, as most small bridges over the country roads had been blown up, and we crossed on the two planks that had been placed for such a purpose.

There were stray animals everywhere, mostly donkeys, these were used as beasts of burden or harnessed to small carts. Once my father came home in

5

a fearful temper. He had come across a man savagely thrashing his donkey because the poor, emaciated beast could not pull the huge load in the little cart.

Daddy, who had an explosive temper when aroused, stopped the car, leapt out, wrenched the whip from the man's hands and proceeded to give him a sound beating before breaking the whip over his knee. He then got in the car and drove off!

My mother did not, at that point, drive a car, but learned the skill in a hard way. One day Daddy had gone to his appointment by train, for what reason I do not know. It was late and dark and there was a tremendous thunder storm raging when an urgent knock came at the door. Kathleen on opening it saw a member of the Garda, and instantly fell on her knees thinking something dire had overtaken "The Captain", as my father was known.

However, the message was that a railway line had been blown up, he could not get home, he had telephoned the police station to ask them to ask my mother to get in the car and fetch him from a distance of some forty miles.

Mother was terrified of thunder storms and used to rush to her bed and hide her head under a pillow once the lightning started flashing. Kathleen it was who dislodged her from under the pillow, and bade her see the officer and learn the route she had to take.

My mother whose determination, courage and steadiness in the face of crises was phenomenal, overcoming her fear of the storm, put on the leather motoring coat that my father had given her in one of his rare moments of affluence, a pair of his driving gauntlets and her brown cloche hat and climbed into the car. That night in pouring rain, thunder and lightning, she not only drove a car for the first time, but through the fearful storm and arrived safely to where my father was stranded.

How she did it no one will ever know, but from that moment on she became a keen driver and was always behind the wheel whenever she could dislodge my father!

We came back on the boat that was full of wounded soldiers from some encounter my mother said, called "Spike Island". She was so busy lending a hand with the nursing that she quite forgot to be sea sick.

CHAPTER
TWO

From West to East

The Gower Peninsula in the early twenties was quite unspoiled. Although I was then four years old I only have hazy memories of the house my parents rented, it was just another one in a terrace and quite unmemorable apart from the fact that from the little window in the loft we could see the Mumbles lighthouse, and Daddy would steal upstairs unbeknown to Mother, or so he thought (there was nothing going on that Mother did not know about!) and take me from my bed up the rickety stairs to the loft to watch the light flashing its warnings to shipping, and tell me stirring tales of the ships that passed along the coast and of the storms at sea and the wrecks that had occurred. He was a wonderful story teller and fired my imagination with the brave deeds of the sailors and their rescuers as well as stories of the smugglers and wreckers. When he was away from home he used to write letters to me and enclose cartoons of funny animals and people that all told a story. I think if he had put his mind to it he could have become a cartoonist as he certainly had a gift for drawing.

The beaches, the cliffs and the woods of the Gower stay in my memory and the lovely times we spent outdoors in idyllic weather. I think we were only there for late spring and summer as Mother and I, and sometimes Daddy, seemed to spend every day on the beach or in the woods.

Langlands Bay was quite breathtaking with wonderful woods full of bluebells growing right down to the beach. Caswell Bay was exciting as it was here we collected the pretty cowrie shells.

My father, being a keen sea fisherman, spent all his spare time with a rod in his hands. I used to trot along with him early in the morning to help dig the bait. This was the lug worm, and we found it by looking for the squiggly worm casts in the sand. Digging down we soon found what we sought and in less than no time my pail was full.

Daddy fished from the beach, and not being a squeamish child, I was happy to help select the choicest lug and watch while it was impaled on the hook. All kinds of fish were caught in this manner, small dabs being my favourite as they made a tasty meal, but when the weather was stormy at sea and big waves crashed on the sands, a good catch of bass was hauled in.

In fine weather Daddy enjoyed swimming quite far out. He was adamant that I had to learn to swim but although he tried every trick, the task was beyond him. I was terrified if the water came higher than my knees and have remained so! Conversely my step-sister was a veritable fish in water and also loved sailing, a pastime, along with swimming, all the rest of the females in the family have avoided like the plague!

What funny clothes we wore to go in the water! Old snapshots show my father in an all-over costume, the legs coming down to his knees, seated in a deck chair with a cap made of a large cotton handkerchief knotted at all four corners, to keep the sun off his head. Daddy was very fair and easily caught the sun. There I am in similar garb, seemingly a size too big, and with my long hair bundled up under a rubber cap, as I was quite happy to lie and splash in the shallows or the rock pools.

There were winkles sticking to the rocks and Daddy and I used to pick a paper bag full and Mother cooked them for me and I had them for my tea, picking them out with a pin and dipping them in vinegar.

Every day Mother made a picnic lunch and we took it to one bay or another. Our idyll however was to be rudely disturbed by a couple who came on holiday with their mentally retarded daughter, about five years older than myself. It was my first encounter with someone who suffered in this way and I was very frightened of her. I do not remember their names but can still see them quite clearly. They appeared middle aged and dressed in dark clothes, the lady with long skirts and a large hat and the man with a high collar and tight tie. The daughter was also dressed in a dark skirt and blouse and did not ever wear a bathing costume or go near the water.

I was told to play with her, but she did not want to paddle or make sand castles but only to wrestle me and as she was very strong I was in mortal fear of her and my happy times on the beach were for some days, at an end.

Daddy had been away at work and did not know what was going on, but once he rejoined us, he took charge and things were put right. My mother had such a kind heart that she would never willingly hurt anyone's feelings and did not quite know how to deal with the difficult situation. Daddy was more practical and forthright and told the people that their daughter was too old and strong to play games with me. They of course, took umbrage and after that either did not come on the beach or else sat a long way off until their holiday ended and they went back to their home.

It was in the autumn that we upped sticks again and moved to Southwold on the east coast of Suffolk, exchanging the warm west wind and sheltered coves for a bungalow on the high cliffs and the bitter wind off the north sea.

My father had several friends who farmed in the area, and as he was a good shot was away a lot at shooting parties, but he did have a job of some sort although I do not know quite what it entailed.

The bungalow was wooden and painted white, it had a veranda and a flight of steps leading up to the flat roof. From here there were wonderful views over the water, and Mother loved to sit up there in the evening with her paint box and easel and paint the reflection of the sunsets in the waves. It was fun to watch all the boats to-ing and fro-ing, but as it was so cold there were few people on the beach, only the fishermen, the occasional horse rider or people exercising dogs.

Every day I was muffled up and taken for a brisk walk along the promenade. I can remember being numb with the cold, my face blue and the sting of the bitter wind making my eyes run.

Winter evenings were cosy by a blazing fire. Mother had a fund of fairy stories at her command and also knew a great many poems and songs. I enjoyed listening to her singing various pieces from Gilbert and Sullivan since in the past and in her better times, she had been a keen Savoyard and had a great love for the music. "Three Little Maids from School", "Tit Willow", the "Cobblers Song" and many more, I could never hear them often enough.

Mother was an accomplished pianist and used to accompany my Aunt Lovey, her younger sister, when she sang at concerts as my aunt had a very fine voice and several times appeared at the Queen's Hall. Mother remembered many of the ballads she had played on her piano in her old home and which were sung in the drawing room in the evenings when she was young, "I hear you calling me", "Oh that we two were maying", "A brown bird singing" and sundry other old pieces joined our repertoire. I revelled in the drama of the Victorian songs which told a story, mostly with an unhappy ending.

Then there were the poems which I loved and learned by heart from hearing them so often. My favourite was "The Jackdaw of Rhiems" from Ingoldsby's Legends, which is both humorous and dramatic, and I was soon reciting pieces from it and in time learned the whole poem. There were also funny poems such as this . . .

> Three old ladies were they, were they,
> Who went for a walk on a summer's day
> One carried a spyglass to look for cherries,
> One carried a ladder to climb for berries,
> While the third, and she was the wisest one,
> Carried an umbrella to keep off the sun.

There were more verses but sadly I have quite forgotten them.

Mother and my grandmother both spoke French and German, so I learned "Sur le pont d'Avignon" in French and both the scary poem "The Earl King" and the Christmas hymn "Silent Night" in German. Both Mother and Daddy, when he was home, read to me every day. "Alice in Wonderland", "Black Beauty", and Mother's favourite, "Strewelpeter", a German book full of horror stories of what happened to children if they did not behave!

I got to know all the fairy stories by heart and in their turn the Beatrix Potter books and later A A Milne but I was very soon able to read these for myself. Best of all was when Daddy told a story that he made up as he went along, they were always funny and had a happy ending.

As I was nearly five my parents thought it time I started school and I was enrolled at a small private dame's school on the sea front. The head mistress was very stern and frightening and the rules were rigid. We did our lessons from nine until eleven and then a ten minute break for milk and a biscuit, then more lessons until twelve forty five when we broke to wash hands and tidy hair before lunch.

After lunch each child was given a small and rather hard cushion and all made to lie on the floor and rest for half an hour, and then another hour's lesson before we were collected by our mothers.

I do not remember much about the school after the first day which is burned in my memory. The lessons I liked as my mother had taught me my alphabet and I could write and read quite fluently for my age, and I could also count and do simple sums. I never drank milk and when I was given the glass, sneaked into a corner and poured it into a pot with a large and dusty Aspidistra growing in it that was the only decoration in the dining room.

Lunch I have never forgotten because of the vegetable marrow, which I hated and was never made to eat at home, probably because mother did not like it either and it seldom turned up on our table.

It was different at school! I said I did not like marrow and that called coals of fire upon my head. Children at this school ate what was put before them, I was told. Long after the other little girls had gone to rest I was still sitting with my plate of marrow before me, cold now and congealing. At last unable to restrain herself any longer, the mistress scooped some up in a spoon, seized me round the head and forcing my mouth open shoved the spoon and marrow in.

14

It was to be my only meal at the school. After that and for the short time I attended, Mother collected me and took me home for lunch.

At weekends Daddy took us out in the car, sometimes as far as Cromer where in early autumn the cliff tops were covered in poppies, and I heard wondrous tales of a whole village reclaimed by the sea and how when the tide was out and the wind blew, the bell of the church could be heard ringing. Mother loved the Cromer trips as there was so much for her to paint.

Sometimes we went to Felixstowe which had exciting games on the promenade; my favourite was the machine that blew coloured ping pong balls in the air and you had to catch them in a net. If you caught a stated number you won a prize. There was a Punch and Judy show, which I hated, as I have always disliked dolls and puppets.

A great favourite with adults and children alike was the man who made sand castles, real castles with turrets and flags on top. He was always on the sands with some grand layout.

I loved the donkey rides and would have happily sat on my ancient steed all day. Ice cream was a treat but Mother would not allow me to have candy floss to eat as she said you never knew what such things were made of!

Visits were made to Yarmouth which was bigger and brasher than Felixstowe and did not have so many delights. My parents always bought bloaters and kippers to take home when we visited Yarmouth.

My favourite trip was to Walberswick because there was a wood carver there who carved the most beautiful animals and birds. My parents bought me some, but over the years and all the moves they have sadly all got lost.

I do not remember which pier it was that Daddy fished from, but I do remember being given my own line with a hook and bait and throwing it down into the water. After a while Daddy said, "Run and get yourself an ice, I will watch your line". So off I trotted and when I got back there was Daddy all excited. I had a bite! Carefully and with fast beating heart, I hauled my line in, and sure enough there was a fish on the hook . . . a kipper! I was delighted, I had caught a fish, at that age I did not know that kippers do not swim about in the water!

One day Daddy caught an enormous cod and carried it home on his back, it was as tall as he was. Mother went to cut it up, but it was just full of sea water and quite inedible.

My parents were great walkers and when we were all together we went out most days. My father was over six feet, ramrod straight from Army days, fair haired with a clipped military style moustache. He was always immaculately dressed and sported a button hole — usually a fresh carnation — wore a trilby hat at an angle and leather gloves, and carried a walking stick. Mother was also tall, about five foot nine, very erect in her carriage, and with an aristocratic nose and piercing hazel eyes. Daddy used to say that when Mummy looked at you, her stare went right through and buttoned up at the back! She too, was smart in a subdued way. Daddy walked with a military step which meant he was always yards ahead of us, so every now and then he would stop, lean on his stick and look up and down the road while waiting for us to catch up. He used to drill me as we walked along. "Left right, left right, pick 'em up there!". I thought it great fun and used to march in step and salute him very smartly. Mother picked flowers and sprays of leaves for the vases. In summer she loved the moon daisies but as she suffered badly from hay fever the flowers caused her to sneeze and cough, yet she would never give up bringing them indoors.

One day we were out walking when a white Bull terrier came up smiling the Bull terrier smile and wagging his tail. He washed my cheeks and fell in beside us accompanying us home. My mother was very worried as she did not know to whom he belonged and had to go back to the shop and ask. "Oh, he belongs to the Sergeant", she was told, so we went off to the police station. Bill, as he was called, did indeed belong to the Sergeant of police, who was a jolly man and thanked us for bringing Bill back. However, when we got home, there was Bill sitting smiling on the doorstep. For the next week my mother spent much time taking Bill back to the police station, only to find him on the step when she got home.

One night there was a very hard frost and when Mother opened the door in the morning, there was poor Bill curled up on the step, stone cold. Mother and Daddy carried him in and set him on rugs before the fire, mother massaged him and I sat beside him and wept salt tears on his head. He was my best friend. Daddy said it was no good, but Mother shook her head at him fiercely when I asked what he meant. And then suddenly the old dog opened one eye and then both and smiled, and not long after was on his feet lapping a bowl of warm milk.

After that the Sergeant said, "Well, Bill seems to prefer living with you, you had better keep him". So we did for as long as we lived there.

One evening just as it was getting dusk there was a great thunder storm. Mother rushed to her bed and hid her head under the pillow, but Daddy and I put on our raincoats and sou'westers and went up on the flat roof. It was a wonderful experience. The sky over the sea was inky black, split every few minutes by jagged flashes of lightning, and as we watched, a skein of white geese flew across the dark background. The thunder crashed and the sky emptied and when it started to calm down Daddy and I, thoroughly exhausted with excitement, scrambled down the steps and got out of our wet things and Mother made us bowls of hot soup, tut-tutting and grumbling at Daddy for letting me get so wet!

One day Daddy told Mother that he was taking me into Southwold for a treat and I was to wear the embroidered frock my grandmother had made me. Mother could not understand why he wanted me to wear this frock and made quite a fuss about it, but he had his way and off we went. He had made an appointment with a photographer for me to have my picture taken, and we went to the studio where I had to stand very still while the photographer crouched behind his camera and disappeared under a black velvet cover.

The photograph was duly presented to my mother as a birthday gift and was much appreciated, and it really was a surprise as I kept the secret of where we had been.

I must have been nearly six when we left Southwold, going quite suddenly as we always did, and Bill had to go back to the Sergeant. As we drove away from the Police Station, Bill suddenly rushed out from a back gate, and I can still see him galloping along in pursuit of our little car. I do not know how far he ran until he realised we were gone for good, I just hope he was not too sad and perhaps found another child on whom he could bestow his love and care. Bill's lovely nature and friendship left me with a lasting affection for Bull terriers.

CHAPTER
THREE

When I Was Seven

The next house in whose front door we turned the key was a tall, narrow and rather grim Edwardian edifice up a quiet road in what was then the very small town of Kelvedon in Essex. My parents had taken furnished rooms there but why we moved to Essex I never knew.

Our landlady was a middle aged, grim faced spinster, who wore brown stuff skirts down to her ankles, severe dark blouses with high necks fastened by a plain broach and had sparse, greying hair pulled back in a severe bun. She was not all that keen on children or animals and made no secret of the fact!

The house itself had a large garden in which I was allowed to play with strict instructions not to damage the flower borders. On one side was a greenhouse in which a few dispirited pot plants endeavoured to survive. We had not been there long when I discovered the rockery that graced the north side of the house was full of snails.

Being of a competitive turn of mind I decided that snail races would be a god idea, so I collected a bag of the creatures and put them in a cabbage-lined shoe box in the greenhouse. Each day when out to play I set up a race course on the floor and with encouraging cries of "Gee up" endeavoured to get the slow creatures to move. It kept me amused for hours. However, all good things come to an end. The landlady decided to collect a couple of the potted plants for transfer to the house and her visit to the greenhouse coincided with the day I had omitted to shut the box lid tight and there were snails crawling about everywhere! I got a good wigging, although I saw my father, purple in the face, trying not to laugh.

To assuage my disappointment over the snails, my father bought me a liver and white spaniel-type puppy as a present. I was enchanted, the landlady was not and made quite a fuss. I called the puppy Dinky and we were soon fast friends, but my first experience of owning my own dog ended only a few weeks later when Dinky escaped through the front door and was run over by the milkman's horse-drawn float and killed.

Across the road was a large walled garden that had once belonged to a manor house, by then pulled down. The garden had been sold and was being run commercially. From our bedroom window I could watch all the gardeners going about their business, and the various dogs that accompanied them. How lucky I thought them.

June, and I suddenly went down with whooping cough. This is a quite unpleasant illness and I was kept in bed and had to amuse myself with books, pencils and paper, and watching the work going on in the garden opposite. Daddy brought me fresh strawberries from there which were delicious, but did not agree with the horrid cough! The landlady was quite annoyed at a child getting ill in her house, and was adamant that my mother should take me down to the local gas works where the smell emanating from such was supposed to act as a sure-fire cure for the disease! I am glad for all of us that Mother resisted her suggestions.

Just after this episode we moved again but not far, this time to a cottage in a terrace at the top end of the town. It only had a back yard, but room to play. My bedroom was above the pavement, and at six o'clock each evening after my mother had wound my long hair up with strips of rags, into what I termed "woggles", I was put to bed. I was allowed to read for twenty minutes and my favourite books were "Little Red Rabbit" about a daring rodent who could climb trees, and "Enid Blyton's Book of Bunnies" in which the rabbits were always outwitting "Wily Weasel" and a particularly evil fox. I have never seen this book mentioned when the author's enormous output is written about, maybe it was one of her first efforts, I remember it as a jolly good read.

Once I had to put my book down, my method of getting to sleep was to sing loudly all the songs mother had taught me. Years later I learned that children used to stop on the pavement outside and listen!

By this time my parents had decided that I should have some more schooling and engaged a governess. Her name was Miss Thorne, but as she was thin to the point of emaciation, my father christened her "Tubby", and Tubby she remained. She was a nice cheerful soul and we got on well although I do not think she taught me a great deal.

Every afternoon, rain or shine we went for a long walk, sometimes down the town and back through countryside, sometimes round the allotments but mostly up the road beside the lovely parkland that no doubt held a grand house in its embrace.

This walk took us over the manned level crossing where the gate keeper lived in a tiny cottage. The hedge round his dwelling was one great mass of purple everlasting sweet peas. He came out as soon as we appeared and insisted on picking a bunch of his flowers for us. I heard Daddy say that he thought that fellow was sweet on Tubby, but this sort of talk passed over my innocent head!

Tubby was a keen photographer and the proud possessor of a Box Brownie. Her interest was in ancient gravestones and we spent much time walking round the local churchyards looking for interesting stones to capture on film.

Mother was always a busy person and a good cook and at the Kelvedon cottage she had time and means to produce enjoyable meals. Roast beef and the lightest of Yorkshire puddings or boiled beef and carrots with huge dumplings were the invariable Sunday dinner. It was called Sunday dinner in those days, Sunday lunch is the modern name.

Mother also made the lightest of sponge cakes, buttery shortbread and melt in the mouth pastry, all of course when the family fortunes were in a fair state. At other times when money was short it was rabbit stew or cod's head boiled and served with egg sauce, while at those times it was only bread and butter and rock cakes for tea!

Both my parents were heavy smokers, Daddy being a 60 a day man. In those days smoking was as social as drinking is today, and at Christmas I remember Players cigarettes in boxes of anything from 25 to 500 being given as presents.

Mother used to do all her cooking with a cigarette in the corner of her mouth, the ash getting longer and longer. I used to watch with fascination to see how long it would be before the ash dropped in the mixing bowl. However, Mother seemed to know the exact moment to flick it in the sink and no ash ever got in the food.

Mother told the story of her brother bringing home cigarettes that one of the boys had smuggled into his boarding school, and how she, at ten and her sister aged eight had sampled them in the bathroom, the window wide open in case someone in the household twigged what they were up to and told their parents! All three smoked heavily all their lives, and my mother reached the age of ninety two, her sister eighty nine and my uncle ninety six, none of their ends being brought about by tobacco!

On summer evenings when midges were biting I used to ask mother to blow her cigarette smoke over me to drive the midges away; it was very effective.

At Kelvedon several more dogs entered my life. My mother, whose passion was Yorkshire terriers, had long expressed a desire to own a puppy of the old established "Pellon" strain. My father had absolutely no knowledge of the breed or indeed of dogs in general, however this did not deter him arriving home one winter's night and taking from his pocket a tiny puppy and presenting it with pride to my mother, along with a large and very grand pedigree stating that the owner of this impressive document was "Pellon" bred! Where he had bought it is unknown, and whether he had been conned is a moot point. Mother was enchanted and I was allowed to choose a name. I settled on Tweedie for no reason that I can remember.

Tweedie thrived and flourished, indeed she grew and grew and by the time she was twelve months was as big as a Cairn terrier! Although she had the correct blue and tan silky coat it was not very abundant and she had drop ears instead of the proper prick ear of the breed. Not any good for show, Tweedie became the family pet, and indeed for the next fourteen years, my friend and companion.

Tweedie however was not the only canine we were involved with at the time. My step-sister Barbara, nineteen years my senior was on the stage, working mostly in repertory. Barbara was a true animal lover and could never resist one that needed help. The trouble was that landladies in theatrical digs were not all that keen on providing a home for displaced rabbits, cats, birds, dogs and so on, so the livestock had to be moved on, usually to my mother!

It was not long after Tweedie's arrival that Barbara came to stay bringing with her the latest hard luck story, a large Airedale terrier bitch called Bijou, rescued from a rag and bone man. Bijou was a charmer and settled down very happily and allowed me to dress her up and would sit in the dolls pram which was never used for dolls, wearing whatever costume I provided for her. However, as the cottage was so small my father decreed that Bijou had to be found a good home and this was done to my great dismay.

Barbara next arrived with a perfectly hideous black and white puppy that looked like a pig. She had brought it back from Jersey where she had been working, having rescued the puppy which was due, with its siblings, to be put down. Babs was depressed that the rest of the litter had succumbed to their fate. Due home, she drugged the puppy on aspirin, fastened it inside her muff and brought it back on one of those dreadful unstable rust buckets that plied between England and the Channel Isles.

It had been christened The Jersey Lilly, but anything less resembling the original owner of the name, cannot be imagined. Happily some dogless soul turned up quite soon to give it a home.

The guinea pigs I was allowed to keep, but mother turned the pet rats down flat. Next to arrive was a tortoise called Tort, and he stayed as companion to one I already owned called Tortie — we were not over given to original names!

Mother was a little concerned that I did not mix with children of my own age. It did not worry me, as I lived in a world of make believe. Like most children I had "make-believe" friends. Mine were a family of cats, the chief of which was "Bluey", and when sitting at table would ask that a second chair be provided beside me so

Bluey could have lunch as well! I talked for hours to the cats, mostly when sitting on the lavatory seat, and they stayed with me for several years.

I also spent much time writing little stories and plays which my collection of woolly animals acted out. A large and constantly expanding farmyard of lead animals occupied me for hours, transporting my stock to market, milking the dairy herd and ploughing imaginary fields. I was reading quite fluently and always had my nose in a book. Add to this my games with the dogs and attending to assorted livestock (I was brought up to feed, water and clean out any animals I owned) and the morning lessons with Tubby and long walks and my time was satisfactorily filled.

Daddy had taught me to play cards and at that time instructed me in the game of Cribbage, which became quite an absorbing pastime when he was home, and a game I have played all my life. There was sixpence riding on each rubber and I seem to remember that when he won I solemnly made out an IOU until the day I received my pocket money! Daddy always paid promptly.

However, all this activity was not enough for my mother who arranged for me to go and play with the little girls who boarded at a small convent situated in the road leading to the level crossing. Although the convent boasted a swing which was delightful, the visits there were not a success as I did not care for the other children and they certainly did not want a stranger invading their settled world. I was, however, invited to their Christmas party and Mother made me a special dress in brown velvet with coffee coloured lace collar and cuffs and bought me a pair of bronze dancing slippers. There was the dreaded Punch and Judy show, a lot of sticky cakes and various games and then balloons and sweets to take home. I was glad when it was all over and I think my parents saw my silent suffering because I was not sent to the convent again.

My step-sister, who was always away from home, counted as a "grown-up", so I grew up as an only child. I am always annoyed when people pity a single child, some onlies may perhaps long to be part of a larger family but personally I never regretted not having siblings or friends of my own age.

One of the joys of Kelvedon was the fact that Mother's cousin, Raymond lived in the same road in one of the large houses. Cousin Raymond was a big, smooth faced man with mild blue eyes and a rapidly balding head. He reminded me of Humpty Dumpty as he had a large egg-shaped head and body shape to match. His wife was a bronze haired, hard faced, smallish woman, whose pet name was "Wopsie", and my father quickly rechristened her "Waspie" which suited her well, as she had a shrewish tongue. She dressed in the fashion of the time, with cloche hats trimmed with cherries, and seemed to be addicted to those loose blouses knitted in silk, brownish, shot through with orange and rather short, flared skirts.

Cousin Raymond was quite wealthy and the house was beautifully furnished and had a staff of maids and a gardener. His hobby was the new thing, wireless, and the house was festooned with cables and speakers, many of which he had made himself and there seemed to be a wireless set, again mostly home made, in every room. I loved to be invited in to listen to Children's Hour, especially "Uncle Mac" who at the end of each programme read out the names of children who had birthdays that day and he instructed them where to look for presents. I especially liked his call of "Hello Twins!".

On my seventh birthday I was invited to Cousin Raymond's for tea, which was laid out in the dining room, but first I was told I could listen to Children's Hour. All innocently I sat absorbed until the birthday slot came and I heard the well known voice saying my name and telling me to go to look in the clock in the hall. I raced out and carefully opened the door of the grandfather clock and there was a pile of gaily wrapped presents. It was a thrill I have never forgotten.

Cousin Raymond had an old terrier dog who was quite blind and had been since a young age. He was a wonderful dog as no one would ever have suspected he could not see. I think he knew every piece of furniture and where it was placed and would sniff for the edge of a chair or sofa before jumping neatly up. I used to have great games with him, throwing a ball which he retrieved and brought straight back to me, just as a sighted dog would.

It was with dismay that I heard my parents discussing the fact that Cousin Raymond had sold his lovely house and was going to live on a boat moored up at Maldon. All the male members of my mother's family were mad on boats and the sea, so I suppose he was just like the rest. Cousin Wopsie was just as keen and there was a grand auction of all their furniture, books and pictures and off they went in their large car, the old dog sitting up between them.

Mother hated boats and never went to see them but Daddy drove me up once to visit. I was amazed at how two people, especially one as large as Cousin Raymond, could fit in such a small boat, and thought it a very uncomfortable way of living. I also hated the way the boat moved all the time and was glad to get off.

Daddy took me to lunch in Maldon and at a little gift shop I spent some saved-up pocket money on a broach for Mother. It was a bunch of violets set against a leaf, I think it was probably made of tin, but well coloured. Mother was so pleased and kept it for years.

Cousin Raymond and Wopsie stayed on their boat for the rest of their lives, and both lived to a ripe old age. They never seemed to miss their former existence. Every now and then Mother had a letter from one or the other of them extolling the virtues of living on a boat and inviting us to visit, but we never saw them again.

CHAPTER
FOUR

Electric Art Shades

My mother, brought up in Victorian days when young ladies were taught needlework, to play the piano, to speak French and to paint, had become proficient in all four skills. However, although she was a most accomplished needlewoman, it was her painting that brought her most pleasure and she became quite a clever artist, specialising in landscapes, gardens, sunsets and flowers. Up until the 1920s she had sketched and painted purely for her own pleasure.

At that time electric light was being laid on to most houses and the only lampshades on sale were made in clouded glass shaped like a coolie's hat. They offended my mother with their stark look and she bought some Raphael Tuck transfers of flowers and birds and stuck them on the shades. My father coming in, looked at them with a shrewd eye and said, "I could sell some of those!". My mother laughed, but Daddy was persuasive, went out and bought half a dozen of the shades, got Mother to decorate them with transfers, packed them up in a small suitcase and set off for London.

The next day a telegraph boy arrived on his bicycle, the telegram he delivered was from my father, it read "Have order one gross of shades". I can see my mother's face now. "Where on earth can I put 144 shades?" she exclaimed, looking round our tiny sitting room. Next day another telegram arrived with two further orders, three gross in all.

My mother, ever a resourceful woman set off that day coming home with the news that she had rented, for five shillings a week, the loft over a stable as a studio and engaged two girls to help her. Tables and chairs were procured and set up in the newly swept loft, the girls plus the shades and transfers were installed and work commenced.

I loved to climb the rickety stairs with Tubby and help clear up the papers left by the used transfers. The girls were jolly and the busy hum of their chatter filled the loft. The orders rolled in and the workforce swelled to six girls and a man who came in daily to pack the shades carefully in the wooden boxes that had been acquired, and convey them by horse and cart to the station.

Mother was never one to get bogged down with one idea. One day when Tubby and I climbed up into the loft, Mother was painting a design in oils on a shade instead of using a transfer. When Daddy took these to show the buyers, even more orders came, and Mother set to and engaged other girls with an artistic bent and showed them how to copy the designs she had made.

About the same time she decided that the shades were heavy and ugly and something lighter and more pleasant to look at could be used to shade the light bulb. She chose as her material, vellum. A local man fashioned, at her direction, two round wires one larger than the other. She bound the wires with tape and sewed it on, and then stitched the cut out pieces of vellum to the wires, covering the stitches with "gimp" which was also stitched on. Then she designed and painted flowers or gardens on the shades. It is believed that my mother was the very first person to make a vellum lampshade.

The orders proliferated and soon the loft could not hold all the work and my parents rented a factory building the other side of the town. In less than no time the workforce increased fourfold. There was the design and painting area, a section where the wires were covered, another where shades were assembled, a packing department and a small office. At its peak there must have been quite a large work force.

Outside there was a lot of spare ground and some sheds and, not liking to waste anything, my mother took up turkey breeding and soon we had a small flock of white turkeys.

The business was registered as "Electric Art Shades", by now selling all over the country. Very soon overseas orders flooded in, even from some of the big stores in New York and the packing department had to deal with an export as well as the home market.

My parents decided on a show to advertise their enterprise, and hired a room in a London hotel where the shades, most in vellum but now some in silk with fringes, made a great display. I was taken up one day and remember the large tables set out with all Mother's best designs and ideas, large and small shades, and by now in all sorts of shapes. The room was crowded with would-be buyers and if only things had gone on as they were, no doubt my parents would have ended up very rich.

Daddy took us both out to lunch at Frascartis in Oxford Street; it was the biggest restaurant I had ever been to and rather awe-inspiring for a small country girl. I remember it was in two tiers and we went up gilded stairs to the top and had a table looking down on those lunching below.

After lunch my mother took me with her to Bourne and Hollingsworth the famous haberdashery, to choose gimp, fringes, tassels and other materials necessary for decorating the shades. She also chose a length of pink organdie to make me a party frock as she said with a smile that Daddy was going to take us away for Christmas as a treat and I should need a pretty dress. I slept in the back of the car all the way home.

Although they were so busy Mother and Daddy had quite a social life and went out in the evenings. At that time fancy dress dances were all the rage. On one such occasion they took Tubby, who was dressed as a balloon girl, imprisoned inside a huge hoop covered in orange and red material, with a similar thing on her head. Mother loved to dress as a French clown, painting her face white and with a huge red mouth and thick black eyebrows and her hair whitened and standing up in three bunches from her head. Daddy went as Charlie's Aunt in long skirts and a bonnet. I hated to see them dressed like this, they were no longer the people I loved and I was glad when the next day came and all the costumes went back to the hire shop, and things were back to normal.

When the success of the factory was at its highest point my parents made a fatal mistake. They were approached by two brothers who wanted to invest money in the enterprise and in all good faith took them as partners. The brothers brought a considerable amount of money in to Electric Art Shades and got my parents to agree to move from their factory to more up-to-date premises in Whitham, a town some miles distance down a long straight road.

It was the time when young men had discovered the joys of speed on motorcycles, no helmets in those days, and my chief memories of that road down which we drove regularly, are of the awful accidents at which my parents always stopped to give what help they could. I used to huddle in the back of the car, aware of the bodies laid out on the roadside.

The factory at Whitham was on the eastern outskirts of the town and next to a large farm which proved a magnet for me and where I spent every waking hour, much to the dismay of my mother who had always hoped (against all the signs!) I would follow her and my grandmother into the world of needlework and painting! Some hopes! I had always been a tomboy, far happier outdoors than inside, and now with a farm to explore I was off at every opportunity.

Tubby had left us for another position at about the time of the factory's move to Whitham and my freedom to spend my time happily on the farm was curbed when it was announced that I was to go to school.

There was a private school at Whitham which was attended by small boys in the kindergarten and girls up to the age of eleven. Two of the girls were the daughters of the Crittal family who were just making their name with Crittals Windows. I was only one term at the school and do not remember much about it, except that we wore gym slips and blue jumpers.

Apart from the farm, my nicest memory of Whitham was the pie shop just down the road from the factory. The most delicious hot sausage rolls and pork pies were made and baked on the premises and could be purchased at two pence and four pence respectively, and the smell of their baking wafted down the road as I ran to get our order. They were quite the most delicious things I have ever eaten.

On November 4th Daddy said we were going to drive to London to visit his cousin who owned the Orange Coaches, one of the most popular of the omnibus companies then springing up. Mother told me years later he was worried at the way the factory was being taken over by the partners and wanted his cousin's advice. We drove down in the dark, I was tucked up in the back sucking sherbet dabs which I had lately discovered and had a battle with mother before she would allow me to have any. The piece of toffee on the end of the little stick when dabbed in the sherbet was most inviting. As we drove along I sang to myself "It's a long, long road awinding" which I had heard on Cousin

Raymond's wireless before he moved. I thought it was a lovely song.

When we got to the outskirts of London the street markets were in full swing, ablaze with naphtha flares and the stall holders shouting out their wares. On every corner it seemed, were ragged children with guys in carts begging for pennies. It was very exciting.

I do not remember either the district where the relations lived or their name, but Daddy's cousin had smooth dark hair, a round jolly face and a thick set body. He had a son a little older than me, who had a small snooker table, and took me off to play, I was thrilled, it was the best game I had yet discovered. However, after half an hour we were called to have supper, and then we drove home very late.

Christmas that year was spent at a grand hotel at Hastings, Daddy had promised us a treat and we certainly got one. The whole place was festively decorated and every room taken by families with children. The dining room was full of surprises, streamers and balloons rained down from nowhere. Things exploded on the table showering us with little presents, there were crackers full of gifts and paper hats. Every meal brought more excitement.

My present list, always headed by "a pony", which I knew I would not get, that year included (amongst the books) a writing case and a handbag. Both were to be found inside the pillow case I hung on the bed end on Christmas Eve. The little writing case, like an attaché case was covered in green leather with a gold pattern on the lid, it contained paper, pencils and a fountain pen and several note pads. It was my greatest treasure, for years holding all my scribblings until it fell to pieces from all the use it had endured. The handbag was of embossed leather, patterned in colour, not a child's bag but a grown up's. I was also given a little umbrella with a duck's head handle and several of the books I had requested.

Mother insisted on the daily walk and we muffled up against a freezing easterly gale blowing off the sea.

"It will be sure to snow madam", said the impressive uniformed commissionaire when we came back and my mother remarked on the cold. He was so right. The snow started to fall, softly at first, on Christmas evening just as we all sat down to a sumptuous dinner. This was one of the few times I had been allowed to stay up, and certainly the first time I had sat down to dinner.

I wore the brown velvet dress that had been made for the Convent party and put away in tissue paper ever since, and the Maitre D who was wonderful with all the children, tucked a little sprig of mistletoe in my hair slide. It was a marvellous evening and I fell asleep almost before I got into bed.

When we got up on Boxing Day, it was to find quite a covering of snow. The hotel staff said they seldom got much snow, being by the seaside, but someone who had heard the weather forecast on the wireless said it was bad inland.

That afternoon there was a party for all the children staying, with some exciting games, lots of surprises and some entertainment by a magician. In the evening there was to be a Fancy Dress parade after dinner. My parents had brought their usual costumes from the hire shop, and I was dressed in the organdie dress mother had made, with pink rosebuds in my hair and went as a "Rose Princess". Both Mummy and Daddy won prizes and I was given a box of chocolates, for what I am not sure.

The next day it was snowing when we left the hotel in the car to drive home and as we turned north the weather got worse. We had to negotiate Biggin Hill and an AA patrol man stationed on the road warned my father not to attempt it as it was to be closed to traffic. Daddy was never put off by a challenge and we slipped and slithered up the hill and he said later ours was the last car allowed up.

I do not know whether the advice Daddy was given when we went to London was responsible for the change in our circumstances, but not long after Christmas Mother said we were going to move house again as they had sold their share of the business to the partners. Years later I learned that they had been badly treated and tricked out of quite a lot of money.

Every time we had a move we never seemed to go straight from one place to another, the interim was filled by a stay at my grandparents' house in the Berkshire countryside. They were my mother's parents and I loved them both dearly. Because we moved so often, none of our dwellings (all rented furnished) really seemed like home, while Foxhill, Granny and Gramps' house, was the one permanent thing in my young life and I was devoted to it and always thought of it as "home".

My grandparents had not really approved of my mother's first husband and they were not too keen on her marrying my father only acknowledging him, rather grudgingly, after I was born. Daddy would drop us off or pick us up, only coming into the drawing-room for tea and never staying a night as other relatives did. This time was no different, off we went to Foxhill while Daddy went back to his brother in Bristol to plan the next move and the next house into whose front door we should put the key.

CHAPTER
FIVE

The Old Vicarage

Sometime in early spring my father fetched us and we drove to our new home in Stowmarket in Suffolk. Mother had been away once or twice, leaving me with Grannie and Gramps, as she said she had to choose furniture and carpets for our next home. I was most excited as we had never had our own furniture before.

The Old Vicarage was a huge house and divided in two, the front half was empty and shuttered and we lived in the back half. My mother said that Milton the poet had lived there when he was being tutored by the resident cleric, and that he had planted the mulberry tree that grew in the grounds and had written "Paradise Lost" while sitting under it. I was not quite sure who Milton was but was quite impressed that he was a poet and that we were living in a house of someone so famous. My mother really went to town on furnishing the house. The rooms were huge and the furniture to fill them was on the same scale.

I realised in later years that Mother's bedroom looked like something from a stage set. It had pale pink walls and a white carpet. All the furniture was white painted wood picked out in gold, and the soft furnishings in heavy watered rose silk.

The kitchen had the very latest in electric cookers, a huge bell like affair that was raised on a pulley to display shelves. Two maids were engaged, a cook and a house parlour maid.

As soon as we were settled mother started to decorate the rooms with her own handiwork. The dining room walls were painted in a cream colour and the curtains were brown silk shot with orange and the carpet was a tobacco brown. My mother, seated on top of a tall step ladder painted a frieze of red and gold Virginia creeper all round the top of the walls. After that she set about the drawing room, only the frieze here was of Wisteria, with swags hanging down each corner. The drawing room was hung with lilac curtains in heavy silk and at one end there was a very large alcove. Mother painted a life-sized lady in a crinoline and bonnet on vellum, cut it out and stuck it on the wall of the alcove and then painted tall delphiniums around the figure. She had lighting fixed which, when switched on, made it look as if the figure was about to step into the room.

One day a strange lady came to ask for donations to some local charity and on entering the drawing room exclaimed: "Ooo Mrs Chard, I do like your "alcahove"!". Of course the word went into the family language and they have been "alcahoves" ever since.

There was a large garden mostly lawn and my two tortoises, Tweedie and Mother's other Yorkshire terriers which she showed when time and money allowed, were joined by two rabbits in a hutch, sent up to me by my grandfather who bred and showed Blue Beverans, a half grown black cat called "Blackie", another of Barbara's rescues and a third tortoise, who joined Tort and Tortie under the name of Tortoise. All three were different sizes and looked rather impressive wending their slow way about the lawn.

Next to the house and only separated by the drive was a large red brick chapel, very well supported on Sundays and the sound of enthusiastic voice singing stirring hymns rang round our garden.

It was only a short walk to the main street and situated some way down was a splendid toy shop. I had saved up five shillings and for some unknown reason I spent it on a doll I saw in the window. I disliked dolls intensely and when I got her home I wrapped her in one of the dogs' rugs and put her in Mother's room on her theatrical skip that she had for years and which always travelled with us holding all our clothes. Each morning I used to tiptoe in, raise the corner of the blanket, stare at the doll and say "DULL!" in a loud voice, and then cover her up again. Do not ask me why I behaved like this, I do not know. Mother got so fed up with this behaviour that one day she gave the doll to be sold at a charity bazaar, and I remember feeling very relieved!

Of course I had to have some schooling so another governess was engaged, a red haired Irish girl we all called "Cossey". The vicar's wife heard we had a governess and asked if we would share her as they had a daughter of my age. So every other day Cossey and I went to the Vicarage where the vicar's daughter Monica joined us for lessons and on the other days Monica came to us. She was a plain, fat girl with braces on her teeth and we had very little in common.

The animal family grew larger as Blackie seemed always to have a litter of kittens and the rabbits were as busy as rabbits can be. I was allowed to keep the money for the baby rabbits sold as pets, to go in my money box. We had also acquired some hens and I collected eggs and dispensed corn daily and never tired of the job. After all, my ambition then was to be a farmer and I thought this task was good preparation, like regularly feeding and cleaning out the rabbits. Anyway my father had said if I did not look after the animals he would get rid of them, and fond as he was of me I knew he would keep his word.

One of my favourite outings was to go with my parents for a day's shopping in Ipswich, although Daddy said it was one of the worst towns in which to drive. We always had lunch at the White Horse Hotel which was very old and had historic connections. On one visit the manager took us all round and showed us the old oak panelled bedrooms in one of which some famous person had been shot at. Only the bullet missed.

Lunch in the big dining room, and I was allowed to choose what I liked, a very rare occurrence as in those days children ate what was put before them. My choice was always the same . . . grilled sole and chipped potatoes! The fish came straight from the coast and tasted delicious and was all crispy and crunchy round the edges. Boiled, roast or mashed potatoes were the rule at home, never chipped, so these were a rare treat.

One day when we had been shopping, Mother and I went to cross the road to the hotel for lunch when a motor cyclist came very fast round the corner and knocked us down. I sprawled in the road unhurt but crying because my little purse had opened and all my three-penny bits I had brought to spend were scattered on the road!

Mother was not so lucky, she had fallen and split an eyebrow on the kerb and was bleeding quite badly. People from the hotel rushed over and we were taken inside and wonderfully treated, the page being sent to gather up my spilled treasure, and a doctor called, who stitched up Mother's eyebrow, which ever after grew crooked.

On Christmas Eve, I and several other children were invited to tea at the Vicarage with Monica and I think we were all rather astonished at the number of presents piled up for her. It seemed they had a lot of relations living overseas and every post brought more parcels. Christmas Day was one of the busiest of the year for her father, so presents were handed over on Christmas Eve and there was a grand opening of these boxes and parcels while the young visitors were there. When I told Mother she said it sounded like showing off to her and I think she was right as the vicar's wife was rather an over-dressed lady with a dominant manner and, as Mother said, "not out of the top drawer"! Daddy muttered something about the vicar's wife having designs on being "Mrs Bishop", but I was ignorant as to what he meant. In my teens when I read Trollope I remembered his words and thought Monica's mother was indeed another Mrs Proudie.

Mother got a key from somewhere and we explored the other half of the house. The rooms were huge and included a ballroom in which was a pile of coal. We had lots of trips to the coast that spring and particularly to Cromer so that Mother could paint from a seat on the cliffs. However, my lessons were not to be too interrupted so the trips were mostly at weekends or holiday times.

Cossey was a good teacher and I was making rapid progress with my reading, and had discovered a great deal more poetry. I was also writing quite long compositions and enjoyed drawing maps. Sums never attracted me, I found it easy to do mental arithmetic but was a duffer when it came to writing it down. Although I liked painting, it was clear that I had not inherited my mother's talent, and needlework bored me stiff. Nature walks were my joy and we came home laden with flowers, leaves and berries either to be preserved or dried and set in an album.

One day in late autumn Cossey told me she was leaving to go and teach in a school. It was a sad parting as we had become great friends. However, a resilient child, I soon got over it and then, quite soon, I realised that the maids were not there either. Mother was lighting the fire in the drawing room, Daddy was carrying coals, and Mother had gone back to cooking the meals.

"Where are cook and Joan?" I asked quite puzzled, and was told they had "gone on holiday". "Grannie's maids don't go on holiday" I piped up but no one took any notice.

I was not to know until many eras later, that Daddy had taken up once more with his shooting friends in East Anglia and they had started him on the slippery slope and he was drinking again. Mother had spent a good deal of the money from the sale of their share in the business on the house furnishing and Daddy's conviviality must have used up the rest.

Then Blackie was nowhere to be found, she was going to have some more kittens and I was told she had gone to a new home. Another day I found the rabbits and their cage were gone, also to a new home, and the three tortoises had buried themselves somewhere in the garden and were not to be found. I was there when a man came and collected the hens, dismantled their house and run and took the lot away. It was all very disturbing.

My parents were preoccupied and spent a lot of time shut in one room or the other, talking in hushed tones. Strange men came and knocked on the door and Daddy spent a great deal of time talking earnestly to them, and I once heard him say "Yes, of course I will settle up, next week at the latest". But when I asked who the men were and what they wanted I was told it was nothing to worry about and to run away and play.

Happily for me we still had Tweedie and mother's other Yorkies and I had my books and toys and soon found something to do.

The end came suddenly, this time there was no going back to the comfort of Foxhill while things were sorted out, this time it was very different.

If is only recently that I have been back to Stowmarket and found that the Old Vicarage is now the Council Offices, the Council having saved it from being demolished to make space for a car park. Apart from having a new piece built on in the same style, the house is much the same although the interior must be altered quite a bit. One of the officials was most kind and indeed interested to know that I had once lived there, and gave me a book on the town with pictures of the house. I walked down onto the back lawn and stood for a moment wondering if Tort, Tortie and Tortoise had surfaced in the spring and if so who had looked after them.

CHAPTER
SIX

Flight

My mother was shaking me gently by the shoulder and whispering, "Wake up darling, we are going for a drive!"

A candle was burning brightly by my bed. "Why don't you put on the light Mummy?" I asked. "Daddy has turned the electricity off" she replied rather too quickly, while she was stuffing my toys and clothes in a suit case.

It was freezing cold outside the house and very dark. My father was loading cases and boxes in an old van, he was so quiet and grim I did not dare ask where our nice car was.

The church clock began to strike the hour and I counted the strokes .. one . . . two . . . three and so on until twelve. The witching hour! I shivered inside my woollen jumper and cloth coat remembering all the things that could happen when the clock struck midnight, like Cinderella running from the ball and suddenly finding all her lovely clothes had turned to rags and only leaving a glass slipper to show she had ever been there. What a strange analogy!

I helped to settle the dogs among the luggage, endeavouring to understand what was happening. My questions about where we were going and why were brushed aside with a "Never mind darling", my mother's favourite answer when stuck for an explanation.

There was little room for the three of us so I had to climb in and travel on mother's lap. Daddy quietly shut the van door and an owl hooted mournfully as if giving us a sad goodbye. The old van coughed and spluttered into life, its dim lights were switched on and creakily we moved off.

The journey was a long one, the van did not go very fast and the faint beam from the lights showed only a short way ahead. At some stage in the trip we stopped briefly to eat the sandwiches Mother had made and drink hot tea from the flask. The moon came out from behind the clouds and lit up the frost on the bushes so that it sparkled like a million tiny diamonds. In the distance a vixen rasped. It sounded more like a laugh. Maybe she was right, for it was many years later before I learned we had done a moonlight flit!

The cottage we arrived at as dawn was breaking was the last one in a terrace of ancient vintage. There was a small sitting room, a scullery and one bedroom. The lavatory was a bucket in a sentry box outside the back door.

The tiny sitting room into which we struggled with dogs, bags and cases was sparsely furnished, there was a small grate and two doors, one leading to the scullery and one to the stairs.

The cottage boasted one oil lamp and one candlestick with a stub of a candle and much congealed grease. The cooking was accomplished in the scullery on an oil cooker. This strange contraption had two metal cylindrical tubes on which saucepans and kettle perched precariously, these tubes were fitted to a flat top with a small oven underneath. It was powered by paraffin and gave off the most awful fumes. On this my mother heated all the water we required and did the cooking.

There was not a lot of cooking to be done as, unlike the full cupboards of the Old Vicarage, the only cupboard, situated in the sitting room, rather resembled Mother Hubbard's. Funds must have been at their very lowest. However, my resourceful mother, somehow managed to keep us fed, mostly on stew, the ingredients for which were grubbed from the little back garden, the last occupants having left some roots and sprouts, together with a wild rabbit purchased from the local poacher for a few coppers.

Washing arrangements were primitive, the old tin bath that hung on the outside back wall being brought into the sitting room for Mother and me each morning, filled with two buckets of water, one hot and one cold, while my father made his ablutions in the same way each evening when I was safely in bed.

The bedroom had a tiny lead-paned window looking out onto the lane and another overlooking the sloping roof of the wood shed. It was the same size as the sitting room and could just hold a double bed and a small truckle bed, a rickety dressing table and a curtained recess in which to hang clothes. There was very little room to move about.

The ceiling sloped to the wall at the back of the double bed and the occupants had to be very careful not to sit up suddenly and brain themselves on the black beam in the ceiling overhead.

All went well with both parents exercising extreme care until one night when two cats started fighting on the sloping roof under the open window. A ghastly shriek and locked in a mad embrace they flew through the window fighting across the bed, round the little room and out again. My father uttering a loud and strange oath, shot up in bed and gave his skull such a resounding whack on the beam that it knocked him silly, and Mother had to revive him with hot tea, there being nothing stronger in the cottage.

I chiefly remember the bedroom for the awful week when all three of us went down with a bad attack of influenza and were immured in bed. There was no question of a doctor, they expected to be paid in those days, so Mother dosed us all with quinine, which in my case did not stay long! I can well remember my mother inching downstairs on her behind, a step at a time, to make us a hot drink and somehow get it upstairs. That we all survived was no doubt due to her fortitude as my father not only had flu but a dose of malaria as well.

Once well again, I thought it was all rather fun, much more so than living in the big house where I had to keep my room tidy, not get in the way of the maids and their work and have lessons with the dreary Monica.

Here there were no maids, no room and no governess, not even any lessons, it was one long holiday.

Arthur was a bonus. He was the eldest child of the local vicar. Arthur at ten was two years older than myself and full of fun and mischief. The village church was opposite the cottage and the Vicarage just down the lane. Arthur and I chummed up when he came home from boarding school at the start of the Christmas holidays.

My parents and I were often invited to the Vicarage for lunch. I can only suppose that the occupants recognised our plight and thought a satisfying meal might be a good way of helping without causing embarrassment.

Once Arthur and I had chummed up, I stayed most afternoons to tea, and afterwards Arthur and I would scamper upstairs and creep into his parents' bedroom, which was over the drawing room. Arthur had a heavy old key on a long string which we let out of the window and tapped the panes of the window, uttering loud groans and hoping to scare everyone into thinking there was a ghost . . . it never worked!

Muffled up against the cold we played on the Vicarage lawns and a spreading cedar tree with low branches provided Arthur and myself with a ready-made climbing frame, a vantage point from which to watch what went on beneath and a hiding place when it was time to be called in for tea. We tied a rope to one of the lower branches and this acted as a swing and also a ladder to get up to the little platform Arthur had constructed from wood found in the stable yard.

We were invited to spend Christmas Day at the Vicarage, this meant we should attend the Christmas Day service in the old church. My father was not a church goer and Mother was off the whole idea having had a fill of church when she was a child and they went three times on Sunday and read improving scriptural books the rest of the day.

I do not know what excuse they made but I went to the service with Arthur and a couple of his younger siblings, their nurse and the vicar's wife. The old church was beautifully decorated with berried holly, ivy trails and vases of chrysanthemums. There were hand bell ringers and the old carols rang out sweetly from a full choir and packed congregation. It was quite a change from the little mission church I had attended when spending Christmas with my grandparents, when there was only one vase of flowers on the altar, a choir who seemed mostly tone deaf and a curate who droned on for a full hour.

Unlike Monica's father the vicar made time to celebrate Christmas Day with his family. There were vast quantities of food, a tall tree flickering with the lights of a myriad coloured candles that gave off that evocative smell of hot wax and warm pine that was so much part of the festivities, presents and lots of fun and laughter.

On Boxing Day we went to the meet of the Foxhounds at the next village, walking there over the fields and startling the large number of hares that lived in them. The vicar rode to hounds and very smart he looked in top hat, black melton cloth and dog collar, quite a romantic figure, I considered. That afternoon we saw him coming home in a slightly dishevelled condition, having taken a crashing fall and landing in a muddy ditch.

All too soon the holidays were over and Arthur went back to school leaving me to my own devices. It was then I became fascinated with the little old church and the gloomy graveyard set about with yew trees and overlooking the wide green fields that seemed to stretch forever. I thought they must go to the end of the world and when one day they were spanned by a giant rainbow I was convinced this was so; when I told my father he laughed and said I could be right.

Soon after Christmas there was a wedding at the church. I hung over the creaky wooden gate of our front patch and watched the guests arrive, all muffled in thick coats, the ladies in sensible felt hats and the men in bowlers, the only signs of rejoicing were the white carnations pinned to their coats.

The groom and his best man arrived on foot, both in tight-fitting blue suits with stiff collars and looking rather scared. The bride, all in white, her face blue with cold, was driven up in a pony trap by her father, a grim looking, florid faced man clad in a black suit and with a bowler crammed down over his ears. Mother said not to laugh, since even as a child I had a highly developed sense of the ridiculous, which at times got me into hot water and on occasions, still does!

Mother said the service would take some time, so we went in and tried to warm up by the meagre fire and then ran out to see the smiling bride and groom walk down the path to the gate while those assembled threw handfuls of confetti over them.

The bride's mother and father climbed into the trap and set off at a smart pace leaving the happy couple and their friends to follow on foot. Mother remarked it was a good job it was not raining.

They were lucky indeed, for rain set in that very night and continued for several weeks. The cottage roof leaked and we had to place buckets and bowls to catch the drips, pairs of shoes left in the bedroom for two days were covered in green mould.

At Christmas my step-sister Barbara had sent me a copy of Palgrave's Golden Treasury of Verse, and I was busy reading all the poems, or at least the ones I could manage, although I did not understand many of them.

The one that took my fancy and caught the imagination for its rhythm and drama was Gray's "Elegy in a Country Churchyard". Soon I was learning passages by heart and took to rambling round the churchyard declaiming Gray in solemn tones, especially when the elderly lady who "did the flowers" informed me that many of the inmates of God's Acre had been farm workers. I was entranced. Here indeed was the written word coming alive, I was in the place where the "rude forefathers of the village sleep". I found it tremendously exciting but also rather spooky and enjoyed the cold shivers that ran up and down my spine as I stood by the crumbling wall and looked across the fields to where "the ploughman was plodding his weary way" home.

There was a giant's grave in the churchyard, marked by a stone at each end, the whole measuring nine feet, but the lady who did the flowers could not enlighten me as to who he was or when he lived.

The wet weather brought another interest. Funerals. The first took place a week after the wedding and was that of a local landowner of some importance. I knelt on the window seat and pressed my nose to the tiny panes to miss nothing of the proceedings. Obviously well thought of, judging by the large numbers who had gathered to see him off, he was conveyed to his last resting place in a glass sided hearse drawn by four black caparisoned and plumed horses driven by a cadaverous man in a long black coat and top hat with black crepe hanging in a sodden trail down his back.

"The paths of glory lead but to the grave", I intoned solemnly.

"Good gracious child, stop being so morbid!" cried my mother. I though morbid was a powerfully good feeling, but I knew better than to argue with mother.

Funeral number two also involved horses for which I had a passion. This was the funeral of a local farmer and his coffin, surmounted by hunting whip as befitted a man who welcomed hounds over his land and followed them twice weekly, was placed on a wagon and driven to church by his carter with his two Shire horses in plain harness, black crepe bows on their bridles and their manes plaited with the same material. Behind the wagon was led the farmer's hunter with boots reversed in the stirrups. "That's going a bit far", muttered my father. "They are only going to church, Daddy" I piped up and he smiled.

The funeral procession was made up of a multitude of friends and relations draped from head to foot in black, the widow wearing a waist length black veil. They were all extremely wet. It was an entrancing spectacle.

The third funeral was on the last day of rain before a fierce frost which set the ground so hard the gnarled gravedigger with the thinning ginger hair and rotten teeth would have been hard put to dig a hole.

This funeral was not a patch on the others. One of the old shepherds had been gathered to his forefathers at the great age of ninety six, and when mother told me how old he was I thought he should really have had a better send off for reaching an age I could not even comprehend.

The coffin was pushed and pulled up the muddy, rutted lane on a hand bier, and rested in the traditional manner under the lych-gate before several burly farm workers hoisted it on their shoulders and carried it into church. Only seven people walked in procession, the old man had outlived nearly all his kin. I was starting to declaim, "Let not ambition mock their useful toil", when mother cut me short and told me to wash my hands for tea.

After the frost came deep snow, covering the fields in a thick white blanket. I took Tweedie for runs in the fields startling the hares from their snow-covered forms and the snow came over the tops of my rubber boots and we both became satisfyingly wet. A large tea tray found in the shed made an admirable sledge and I careered, shouting with joy, down the slopes with Tweedie running wildly and barking her delight.

In early February, Mother was making plans to take two of her dogs to Cruft's Dog Show. I was to learn over a lifetime of shows that keen exhibitors do not let such small things as lack of money or transport stand in the way of their show going!

I am not sure how Mother found the cash for entry fees and the train fare, but somehow she did, and in the early morning of the show, Daddy got the old van to start (quite a feat, as it had not been used much owing to them having no money for petrol). Daddy was to go off somewhere that day and so I went to my first Cruft's with Mother. In those days very few children accompanied exhibitors to shows, so I was something of a rarity.

It was still bitterly cold, a thick mist hung over the countryside and in the headlights a fox ran across the road. "Going back to his lair", I remarked in a smug tone.

"About the only thing on this road with any sense!" snapped my father. But mother and I were in buoyant mood and started to sing,

Old Mother Slipperslopper jumped out of bed,
And out of the window she popped her head,
Shouting "John, John, John, the grey goose is gone,
And the fox is away to his lair O'!

I think Daddy was quite pleased when we reach the little station which was busy with other people and their dogs all going to the show, it was very exciting.

Cruft's Dog Show was held in the Agricultural Hall at Islington, a huge, cold barn of a place that smelt strongly of the farm animals that had been exhibited not long before. There were even heaps of uncollected dung piled by the big double doors.

The thick London fog seeped through the gaps in the doors which sagged sadly on huge hinges and mingled with the smoke from pipes and cigarettes making a thick haze; it was rather like looking through a gauze curtain. I was delighted with the scene which infected me with the showing bug from which I have not ever been cleansed!

The boxes of puppies were delightful, in those days there were classes for litters. I was not to know that many of these puppies caught distemper at the show and perished soon after. I fell in love with a box of blue roan Cocker spaniel puppies and vowed that when I grew up this was the breed I would have. Nine years later I was have the first of many Cockers.

A stout bearded gentleman in a trilby hat, cocked rakishly over one eye, accompanied by a rotund lady in a long dress and elaborate toque, were touring the benches. People were smiling and bowing to them and I asked mother in a hushed voice if they were the King and Queen. She laughed and told me it was Mr and Mrs Charles Cruft.

Mother's dogs won two prizes, which was highly satisfying to her and no doubt made up for all the scrimping and saving she had done to enable her to enter and take us on this momentous trip, which was to shape my destiny.

Easter was fast approaching, Arthur would soon be home, I shivered with excitement at the fun we would have. And then suddenly it was all over.

Daddy had been away for a week, he came back looking happier than for months. We were to leave the cottage, Mother and I were to go to my grandparents again, but only for a short time until Daddy found us yet another house. Before Easter came we had left the little Hertfordshire village forever.

CHAPTER
SEVEN

The House
That Was Home

The frequent crises that overtook my parents during my childhood were cleverly concealed from me. As far as I was concerned, moving was a quite usual thing, we did it so often that it became a way of life. However, all children like one safe and secure base and this I had in my grandparents' house set in what was then the heart of the Berkshire countryside.

Every upheaval and change of address was punctuated for Mother and me by a stay at Foxhill, until my father had got things straightened out and we could all be together again in some new dwelling.

I spent so much time at Foxhill until I was around seventeen years of age, that it was home to me, at least I always considered it so, the many places at which we alighted and stayed a while, were interludes. The truth about our many changes of address I did not learn until I was an adult, and Mother, over the years, gave me some idea of the troubles they met and overcame.

We left the cottage in Hertfordshire one March morning when a brisk wind was blowing and the first green shoots were appearing in the woods. Even the old church looked quite cheerful and the spring flowers were already booming in the churchyard.

Daddy put us on a train to London, which we crossed by taxi, a sign that things were better, and caught the westbound train at Paddington. We were going home!

The trains came and went with a great deal of huffing and puffing, clouds of smoke filled the station with that peculiar acrid odour that steam trains emitted; it all added to the excitement. A myriad of porters scurried about and one, for a modest shilling tip, carried our bags to the carriage and saw us comfortably seated.

I always found the journey to Reading thrilling, there was so much to see on the way. First a glimpse of Windsor Castle, then the river at Maidenhead and Mother's tales of when she was a girl staying with relatives who had houses near the Thames and the parties and picnics they all enjoyed. Poor Mother, she sighed so much for the lost and plentiful days of her youth when life was sweet and uncomplicated.

Nearing our destination it was to delight in the brightly coloured fields of flowers at Sutton's Nurseries, the towering red-brown bulk of the Huntley and Palmer's biscuit factory, and a glimpse of the Forbury Gardens, where, one of my story books told me, in the times of Henry 8th, the "good old Abbot of Reading was dragged round on a hurdle". I had not, fortunately for my mother, got round to spotting the prison or discovering the "Ballad of Reading Gaol", that actually came later!

The village taxi driven by the invaluable Mr Smith always collected us from the station, and the eight mile journey was firstly down the Old Bath Road, famous in past centuries for its highwaymen, until we turned off left at the Old Kennels and drove through the little hamlets to the village proper and then up the steep hill to the Common.

The sight of the Rising Sun on the corner opposite the turning to Foxhill always brought the excitement to a head, and as the taxi pulled up at the white gate, Grannie and Gramps were on the steps ready to come down and walk along the path under the rose garlanded pergola, Michael the Sealyham at their side, to welcome us. We were home!

Why was Foxhill so precious to me? Looking back it was probably the orderliness of life there. My grandmother ruled the house with the proverbial iron hand in a velvet glove, and the weeks and months and years unfolded in an orderly manner.

My grandfather lived mostly in his beloved garden and with his animals, coming in only at the prescribed times for lunch and tea, and settling down after dinner at seven to a pleasant hour or so with a detective novel and the racing pages of the Daily Telegraph.

I had few friends of my own age anywhere we lived, so Foxhill was no different. An occasional chum was Peter Lake who, like Arthur, was at boarding school, so I only saw him if we were there during school holidays. He thought I was frightfully lucky as I had no regular schooling, only a sort of hit and miss association with the educational establishment.

Peter's parents had a delightful red brick, tile hung house set in beautiful gardens, both parents being keen horticulturalists. The whole was bisected with little twisting paths which ended up in exciting and unexpected places, like the deep pool where unidentified fish swam and occasionally came to the surface to blow bubbles, the primula garden, the waterfall, and the bamboo "forest".

At one time Peter had determined, as did most small boys of that period, to be an engine driver on the Great Western Railway, so we played railways interminably. A number of large cardboard boxes were tied one behind the other with string "couplings". Peter was in front sporting one of his father's caps. He was the driver and pulled the train, I was the guard, running behind blowing a whistle and waving a piece of green silk tied to a bamboo cane. We made stations all round the garden and passed many happy hours in this fashion, the whole enlightened by a plentiful supply of cake and lemonade from the "Station Buffet" as Peter called the kitchen!

I was always happier with boys for friends than girls, who I found tedious and spiteful. In later years I heard that Peter had "got religion" and become a missionary in Africa, strange how one's childhood friends turn out.

The key to the front door of Foxhill was a large wrought iron object and kept in the drawer of the hall stand, from where each night it was abstracted by my grandfather, who locked up. During the daytime the key lived in the drawer as the house was very rarely left without occupants, two maids being employed, and in those days there was little fear of people breaking in during daylight hours and invading one's privacy. Except in exceptional cases an Englishman's home was indeed his castle.

Nothing much happened at Foxhill that people would imagine could interest and amuse a growing child. How wrong! I spent hours in the garden with Gramps, gardening and helping with the animals. In autumn and winter I borrowed the cook's bicycle and followed the foxhounds, throwing the poor bike over gates and pedalling wildly across grassland to be up with the action and see the hounds working.

The horses and riders provided much enjoyment and merriment, especially the large gentleman with the red face who rode a sturdy heavyweight and tore through each hedge, rather than jumping it, shouting rude words at the top of his stentorian voice. He was closely followed by his fat wife bumping about on her side saddle, her face as florid as that of her spouse's but covered discretely by a large veil which anchored her bowler hat in place. I heard the grown ups talking about these two after hounds and their followers had trotted past the house one morning, and they were referred to as "the Lord Lieutenant of the country and his wife". I had not idea what such a title meant but wondered why, if they were so grand, they looked so funny!

Then I was fascinated with the wild birds, flowers and moths and butterflies and with pond life, and spent hours at pools on the commons or in the woods, fishing out newts and tadpoles.

Accompanied by Tweedie I traversed the woods in spring and summer, picking bunches of wild flowers for Grannie and Mother, and climbing any tree that looked exciting. I knew all the commons and woods like the back of my hand.

That was the great attraction of Foxhill and its surroundings, it never changed, whenever we went back I could be assured that the house still ran on the same oiled wheels, Grannie would be sitting on her sofa doing her embroidery, knitting or making lace on a "pillow". Meals would be on the table at the same time each day, Gramps would be doing the same things in the garden and the countryside I love would be still there. Foxhill meant security, something so lacking in my childhood with my parents. The key to the door of Foxhill was the most precious of all. So much of Foxhill stayed in my memory that I wrote a book about it, "A Door to All My Rooms" which has fascinated countless readers.

CHAPTER
EIGHT

The Sea and the
Forest

The bungalow stood at the crossroads, it was painted white and had looped chains round the tiny front garden, for that reason it was called Chain Cottage. Like most of our dwellings it was very small with one sitting room, a bedroom, kitchen and (luxury!) a tiny bathroom. We also had electric light and after the old cottage and its many inconveniences, my mother was delighted.

I did not think it was nearly so exciting as the shadowy old cottage in Hertfordshire, with its smoky oil lamp and bathing in the tin tub by the fire.

At Chain Cottage we had a nice little garden so Mother was able to enlarge her dog breeding enterprise and acquired several more Yorkshire terriers and also boarded a few dogs, having converted a large shed into two kennels. Mother was a dab hand at carpentry.

The cottage was situated in Hampshire and lay half way between the small town of New Milton and the rapidly growing seaside village of Barton on Sea. It was only a mile to the sea and my parents bought me a second hand bicycle and I was off exploring.

Holidays do not last forever, and it was about a year since I had had any schooling, so my parents sent me to St. Christopher's, a day school for girls, situated on the outskirts of the town and easily reached on my bicycle.

We wore scarlet blazers and red and white checked gingham dresses and panama hats. The head mistress was German, Miss Luwig, tall, gaunt and fierce, her hair drawn back in a tight bun and rimless glasses perched on her beak-like nose. She ruled her little kingdom with a hard round ruler, which she was never loath to use on the knuckles of any girl she thought slacking, being cheeky, talking in class or generally behaving in a manner considered unbecoming.

Although little blue enamel stars were handed out for achievement (I found my one and only carefully wrapped in a scrap of tissue, in my mother's belongings after she died) we were far more likely to feel the ruler or get detention for some real or imagined transgression.

As I enjoyed learning and books I settled in quite happily but did not make any friends. Although I got on well with the other girls while at school, I did not see them at weekends or in the holidays. Instead I met and chummed up with Peter Goddard whose father was in business of some sort. They lived in a large bungalow on the avenue leading to the sea and just over the crossroads. We were joined by two young boys, scions of the Wills tobacco family who lived on the road leading to the town, and Jane Peyton the daughter of a local solicitor who lived next door to them. Both families had large houses and gardens to match. All of these children were at boarding school so we only met up in the holidays.

Our favourite playground lay behind Jane's house, it was a farmer's field and in the centre was a large, old chicken house, the roof of which had fallen in. This became, by turns, a pirate ship, Aladdin's Cave, a train, a fort, a ranch, even a school, as the fancy took us, and we invented marvellous games around this unlikely structure, which kept us amused for hours.

On hot days we cycled down to the beach where all the families had beach huts. Armed with packets of sandwiches and bottles of lemonade we paddled and fished for shrimps, played cricket, climbed the little sand dunes and invented games until it was time, reluctantly, to start for home. On many of these trips we were accompanied by Tweedie and dogs belonging to the other families. All joined enthusiastically in our games and loved to chase sticks or balls into the water, emerging dripping wet and shaking all over us.

At weekends Daddy drove Mother and me into the New Forest to satisfy my pleas to go and see the ponies. We had tea at the Copper Kettle at Pickett Post, demolished many years later to make way for a new road system. I paddled and fished for minnows in the quiet stream at Balmer Lawn, a place that in August now resembles Blackpool.

Sometimes we took lunch in a picnic basket and walked into the Forest. Mother's favourite spot was called Queen's Bower, but one day meeting an old forester he informed her that it was where the adders gather "to hold their parliament", we never got her to go there again! Soon after she received this unsettling news there was a piece in the local paper about a tramp who fell asleep in the Forest and woke up to find young adders crawling in and out of his pockets, he had stopped to rest where a clutch of snake eggs was just hatching. After this story my mother went off the Forest in a big way!

Daddy and I continued our visits, one of my favourites was to Rufus Stone, which seemed a really exciting place, with the story of William Rufus getting shot by an arrow on this very spot. I used to stand with my eyes tight shut hoping that somehow I would be transported back in time to see what actually happened.

"Children of the New Forest" became my favourite book and I longed to live in a hut deep in the Forest and take a deer to provide food which I would cook in a big pot over an open fire.

Sometimes we drove to Christchurch and traversed the road I think was called the Floral Mile as it had banks of beautiful rhododendrons on each side, right up to the town itself.

We also went farther afield along the coast and once stood on the cliffs to see some planes zoom overhead; Daddy said we were watching the Schneider Trophy race. Visits to that part of the coast always resulted in the purchase from fishermen of crabs and lobsters, favourite food for us all.

Sometimes we went to Beaulieu where Daddy told me of the great old ships that had been built there with oak felled in the Forest, it was all so romantic.

Daddy was a great film fan and he and I went to "the pictures" whenever he was home. Daddy always bought half a pound of "jujubes", fruit gums that were our favourites, and we chewed rapidly through the thrilling adventures of Tom Mix, Jack Holt, Douglas Fairbanks and Rin Tin Tin, and laughed at Buster Keaton and Felix the Cat, but neither of us like Charlie Chaplin.

Sometimes the film was chilling and I still remember being transfixed by "The White Hell of Pitz Palu", where a dead man began tapping with his ice pick at the ice frozen over the pool where he had drowned. It gave me nightmares for a week!

When home from school I helped Mother with the dogs, taking them out for walks and cycling up to the town to buy dog biscuits. Mother used a brand called "Osoko" which came in seven pound cotton bags, and I had to buy two and tie one on each side of the handlebars. It was very difficult cycling home as I often got into a wobble and sometimes fell off. When Mother went to a dog show I looked after the dogs left at home, feeling very important and business-like as I did the feeding and exercising.

Mother got to know a local breeder of Yorkshire terriers. Her name was Mrs Shoesmith and she lived in a large bungalow in a very pretty garden quite near the town. She was a very large lady and her face was florid, my mother said she suffered from some skin complaint, Daddy said no doubt caused by letting her little dogs lick her face, which they did all the time, but Mother pooh-poohed the idea. We used to go up there for tea, and I liked playing with the dogs in the garden and enjoyed the nice cakes Mrs Shoesmith provided, but I never liked her, possibly because my father disliked her so much!

Although I never knew anything about the family reverses, I was old enough to sense when things were not going too well, and after nearly a year at Chain Cottage I was told we were to move again. I left St Christopher's and Mother and I and the dogs went back to my grandparents. This time it was only about a month before my father wrote and said he was coming to collect us, as everything was fixed up.

I asked Mother where we were going and she said back to the same place only a different house, this one was situated down the avenue leading to the sea. The house was to be much larger and she and Daddy were going to turn it into a private hotel. Quite how all this came about I never knew, but I think each time Daddy went back to his home city of Bristol, he was able to get a little financial help.

Adults did not, in those days, discuss their affairs in front of children, so it was only in overhearing odd scraps of conversation that I realised that my grandparents thought the whole hotel idea a recipe for disaster.

However, Mother was ever optimistic, for her there was always going to be a pot of gold at the end of the rainbow, Daddy was going to abstain, and everything would be lovely. Poor dear. She was so often disillusioned and disappointed, had to carry all the troubles and worries that came our way and try and settle all the bills, as well as coping with my father when he went off on one of his sprees. It was only when I was grown up that I learned how hard life had been for her.

CHAPTER
NINE

The Avenue Hotel and Boarding School

The new house was a large square dwelling with a half moon shaped lawn surrounded by flower beds in front and a wide gravel drive. At the gate was a dark green notice board with "Avenue Hotel" painted in gold.

At the rear of the house was a large overgrown vegetable garden, which my father was always going to cultivate but never did. It backed on to a field in which a local farmer turned his carthorses and I soon made friends with them.

There were several bedrooms, some for paying guests, Mother and I had one, and Daddy was relegated to a small back room on the ground floor.

My mother told me in after years that he was drinking heavily, and when asleep would snore loudly and shout out as he dreamed, and Mother apparently thought there would be less chance of him disturbing any guests if he was downstairs. I remember the shouts and snores coming from the room and wondered why Daddy made such a noise when he was in bed.

Mother kept the place going by turning the dining room into a restaurant and doing all the cooking. We seemed to have plenty of custom and most of the guests, although grown ups, were very nice to me.

I remember Major and Mrs Pickard who were regulars. Unfortunately the Major was one of Daddy's drinking companions, which was no doubt why my mother was always so distant with him, although unfailingly polite. Mrs Pickard was very outgoing and modern, with the latest style in clothes, a great deal of make-up, red hair which my mother said was achieved by the use of "henna", and a loud and unmusical voice. They came to dinner several nights a week bringing various friends and were some of the best customers to the hotel.

Another couple, friends of the Pickards, also regulars to the dining room, were Mr and Mrs Ferrier Kerr. No one quite knew how to pronounce the "Kerr" and the lady used to get very angry unless it was pronounced "Car". She, like Mrs Pickard, aimed to be fashionable and both ladies, who were into middle age, aped fashions of the young and I once heard my father describe them as "two old muttons dressed as lamb".

Fancy dress dances were still the rage and the Pickards and the Ferrier Kerrs were in the thick of the fun. They persuaded my parents to hold a fancy dress dinner in the hotel dining room, and as there was no room for dancing after the meal they all went on to another location. I watched all the comings and goings from a vantage point on the landing, marvelling at the costumes and the noise grown-ups could make at a party.

Often for these dinners and other parties, my mother and father were invited, and Mother insisted they accept as it was good for business. They usually went in their favourite costumes, she as the French clown and he as Charley's Aunt, and often won prizes, for Daddy a bottle of whisky which was the last thing he should have been given, while for my mother a box of 100 Players cigarettes. I was always hopeful that she would get such a prize as I was an avid cigarette card collector.

One morning my mother and the daily cleaner were in the dining room when I heard fearful screams. I was brushing Tweedie on the lawn and both of us rushed in. The cleaner was standing on a chair white faced, it was she who was making all the noise. "A rat!" my mother exclaimed, "it came out of the fireplace and ran up the curtains. Look, it's on the pelmet!"

I looked up and sure enough there was a large brown rat running along. Tweedie also saw it and started barking frenziedly. This alarmed the rat, who raced down the curtains and across the floor, just missing Tweedie's open jaws, and bolted up the chimney.

The cleaner, who by now was having a fit of the hysterics, was helped off her chair and ran staggering out of the room and was never seen again; mother said she did not even come back for her money, they had to post it on!

Tweedie took up a position by the fireplace and nothing could budge her. All stiff and protesting, she was carried out at intervals into the garden to relieve herself. As soon as she had obliged, she raced back to her vigil. Mother locked the dining room door and hung a notice on it saying that it was closed for redecoration and meals would be served in the lounge.

For two days Tweedie neither ate nor drank and as far as anyone knew she did not sleep either. But she won in the end. The rat, no doubt getting desperate for water and food, must have ventured down the chimney in the night, because on the third morning it was dead on the mat with teeth marks in its throat. Tweedie lay curled up beside it fast asleep. It was the only rat we ever saw there and no one ever found out how it got indoors.

With no school to distract me and a bicycle to convey me, I lived a very happy life for a while. Once a week I cycled up to the town to visit Woolworths, then a threepenny and sixpenny store, and spent my pocket money on exercise books in which I wrote plays and poems and stories.

I had been given an old wind-up gramophone, which was my pride and joy, and sometimes I bought a sixpenny gramophone record. My choice of music for a ten year old must have seemed a bit odd. I loved marches and stirring songs and treasured a copy of "The Stein Song". My actress step-sister sent me a record of the drinking song from "The Student Prince" in which she was appearing, which became a firm favourite. I also like sad songs and loved Irish melodies, my favourites being "Kathleen Mavourneen" and the "Kerry Dances", both of which I played so often that my parents begged me to give them a rest. Another treasured record bought from Woolworths was "Happy Valley", which had a dreadful sickly song call "My Mother's Eyes" on the reverse side. Another favourite record was "Just a Song at Twilight", with "A Brown Bird Singing" on the flip side. I think most of these got worn out from use, I am sure my parents were relieved!

Sometimes my cousin Paddy rode his motorbike over from Bryanstone at Blandford, where he was at school, to spend the day with us. He was always fun but a great tease and loved to take my records and bowl them from the top of the front steps across the lawn, where they ended up in the bushes.

"They won't break!" he laughed at my loud wails and indeed they did not.

On one occasion Paddy arrived in a bad state, his coat all covered in mud, his trousers torn and a large gash in his leg, bleeding profusely. He had had a crash with the bike. Mother swiftly had him up to the bathroom and bathed and bandaged the injury and was begged, almost on bended knee, not to tell her sister about the accident, he was so afraid his mother would forbid him to ride the bike in future. Mother was a splendid aunt, and never said a word to Aunt L until years afterwards, when they both had a good laugh.

As I had not been to school since leaving St Christopher's, it was decided I had better have some more education. I had, by then, become an avid reader of books about girls at boarding school. I think Angela Brazil was probably to blame for my longing to join this elite band! I begged and implored and at last they gave

79

in and I was enrolled at the High School for Girls in Salisbury. I am glad to say this establishment is long defunct and the premises demolished.

Why they chose a city school for a country child I do not know, probably the fees were not as great as the out of town schools. I had to have a large amount of clothing and also sheets and towels and my grandmother sent me six hand towels with my initials embroidered on them and two pairs of linen sheets, all bordered with her hand crocheted lace.

My clothes included a white coat and skirt, the latter accordion-pleated, which was for church on Sundays or any other important occasion. I did not visit the school before my parents deposited me there at the start of the Whitsun term, and it all came as a bit of a shock.

Where was the gracious house, spreading lawns and luxurious playing fields I had read about in my books? Where was the cosy dorm where midnight feasts were held? Where the bunch of girls of my own age who were such fun and up to all manner of japes? And where the smartly dressed and charming mistresses? Well may I have wondered!

The school was situated on the northern outskirts of the city opposite a church and consisted of several Victorian terrace houses, all converted into one. There were around 200 day girls but only 17 boarders, of ages ranging from 10 (myself and the youngest) to a kind girl called Deirdre who was 16 and was my source of refuge during all the miserable three months of my stay.

My introduction to the headmistresses, of whom there were three, filled me with dread. They were sisters and of the three only one had been married and was widowed in the Great War. She was tall and spare and had kind eyes and wore her hair in the fashionable earphones. She was always nice to us and would have done more for us if she had not been overruled by her formidable sisters.

The other two were enormous women, very alike, they could have been twins, with large oval faces, little mean blue eyes like marbles, and I never saw either smile. They wore their greying hair scraped back in buns and dressed in blouses fastened at the neck with cameo broaches, and long skirts almost down to their ankles. Their rule was law.

At the rear of the school was a concrete yard where we played at break time, and did drill twice a week. The playing fields were up a lane beside the church and were rough and, I heard my parents saying, rented from the council. We played rounders that term and it was about the only thing I enjoyed.

The "dorm" was quite a small room into which five single iron bedsteads were crammed and there was a small chest each for clothes and one communal wardrobe. The beds were separated by flimsy curtains. I cried myself to sleep for the first week and got dreadfully tearful each morning; this was where Deirdre became such a comforter.

The classroom of the form in which I was placed was wood panelled; it seemed dark, huge and high. There were rows of desks and the mistress taught from a raised dais in front of a large blackboard. Owing to my scrappy schooling I was miles behind the other girls in many subjects, although I read far more fluently than some and had no trouble with compositions or dictation, and my upbringing in the countryside and familiarity with its plants, birds and animals stood me in good stead during nature study lessons. My knowledge of poems and delight in reciting when asked, pleased the young English mistress who always looked frightened and froze when one of the headmistresses came in to see how we were progressing.

It was in mathematics I fell down. I had never had even a nodding acquaintance with algebra or geometry and my arithmetic was poor, and here incurred the wrath of the maths mistress.

Maths was conducted by a tall, angular, craggy-faced Scotswoman with bright red hair wound into two tight earphones on either side of her head, giving her the appearance of a particularly angry ram. She ruled the class with a waspish tongue and one of those round rulers. She was not keen on giving help, expecting the class to understand at once and brooking no ignorance of her directions. She tapped the black board furiously as she spoke.

I had been there about a month and she was undoubtedly getting exasperated with me, when I dared to put up my hand and at her snapped "Yes?" said I did not understand the lesson. She stormed down from her pinnacle, strode up to me and brought the ruler down on my knuckles. My fiery temper flared and, with a purely reflex action, I leapt to my feet and punched her hard in the stomach! She gave a great gasp and turned a funny shade of purple, there was a dead silence in the room, and then she dismissed the class.

I was not sent for to the headmistress's study, instead I believe they telephoned my parents to remove me. However, sadly for me, this did not come about and I was reprieved and had to write out dozens of verses from the Bible for several evenings as a punishment.

One afternoon each week was the sewing class. This was overseen by the married sister who read us interesting stories as we worked. Most of us were put to hemming seams in enormous cotton knickers for the other two sisters. Looking back, my needlework was such that whoever wore the pair I sewed probably fell out of the seams!

Meals were taken in the dining room, furnished with long bare wooden tables and hard chairs. The food was almost inedible. Lumpy porridge for breakfast, the only eggs we ever saw were on Sunday when we each got one, soft boiled and horribly sloppy. The meat was tough and fatty, sausages made of beef and overcooked, they had a most suspicious taste. The potatoes were always par-boiled and hard in the middle and the only vegetable, boiled cabbage, all wet and soggy.

Several days a week we had to endure boiled suet puddings. These were made with butchers' suet and it was undoubtedly rancid. The stench all through the school as the puddings boiled was appalling. These horrors were served with plum and apple jam or sometimes sugar, and even with this topping, tasted disgusting. When no one was looking, we used to hastily wrap the slices in our handkerchiefs and push them up our knicker legs, after the meal, there was a rush to flush the pudding down the lavatory before anyone caught us!

Tea was thick slices of bread and margarine. Only on Sundays did we see cake, this in the form of an iced bun each.

Monday mornings, one of the sisters came round with a jug of Senna pod tea, and every boarder had to drink an egg cupful, whether they required it or not. Those fortunate souls who have never had to take this noxious stuff do not know how awful this exercise was and how dreaded by all.

On occasional Saturdays we were allowed to walk down the road to the row of little shops and the post office, to buy stamps or sweets with our pocket money. I can remember once spending all my money on a bag of gooseberries as I was so missing all the fresh fruit which I enjoyed at home.

On Sundays, all wearing our white coats and skirts and panama hats we were marched in a crocodile across the road to the church. One Sunday we were taken down to the Cathedral for a special service.

On Sunday afternoons, we went to one of the classrooms and wrote a letter home. I poured out my woes in the first few and wondered why, when letters came from my parents, they asked why I had not written. I learned that all our outgoing letters were read by the headmistresses and those that had any complaints in them were burned!

I went home at half-term and told them how I hated the school, elaborating on various aspects of life there.

Mother, who was used to my vivid imagination, was not impressed and in spite of my pleas not to go back to the school, I was told not to be silly. Daddy took my side but Mother was adamant, she would never listen to Daddy, especially when he was on one of his sprees, and considered that he spoilt me anyway.

When I had been back at school a couple of weeks, he came one Saturday to take me out. I was told by one of the mistresses that I had to take another of the younger boarders with me so I chose the only one I did not thoroughly dislike, a boring girl of twelve whose parents were in India. Daddy was very flushed and his speech slurred. I hugged him and cried and begged him to take me home. He was visibly upset but told me to "brace up".

We went to the pictures to see one of the very first "talkies", I wept silently all the time. Tea at a tea shop was not much better, I could not eat anything. When he left, he said he would speak to Mother. He did. Mother told me years afterwards he was so drunk when he got home she did not believe him, so no release came.

When I went home at the end of term everyone was shocked at the sight of me. From a healthy, happy, rosy cheeked child, I had become painfully thin, huge eyes staring out of a wan face. The doctor who Mother took me to tutted and said I lacked nourishment and had obviously fretted and suggested at least six months before any more schooling. To me he was a saviour.

My clothes and linen were never collected from the school, I think parents were supposed to pay a term's fees if a pupil left abruptly and no doubt by then mine had not that sort of money to give away. Perhaps the school accepted the goods in lieu!

This traumatic experience failed to impress on me that not all you read in books or papers or see on the screen is true to life and I continued to romanticise many aspects of life I had not experienced at first hand, coming down to earth each time with quite a bump.

That summer I was as free as a bird and spent most of the time on the beach with the friends I had made when we were at Chain Cottage. We paddled and built sand castles, played with the dogs, climbed the sand dunes, picnicked and generally enjoyed ourselves. Those who swam did so, but I found swimming quite beyond me and stuck to the shallows.

My step-sister came home in September. She and my father had never hit it off and one night after I had gone to bed there were raised voices and then a loud crash, silence followed by someone crying. It turned out that my father had come in very much the worse for wear and sat in the lounge seeing things. My step-sister went to the wall-mounted 'phone to ring the doctor, and my father flew into one of his rages and tore the 'phone off the wall and threw it on the floor. My step-sister left the next day and my father went out and did not come back for two days. When he did he was quite normal.

I was always worried about the untended back garden. My grandfather had drilled into me how important it was to keep all gardens well dug and planted and to see this wasteland seemed wrong.

One day I was out on my bicycle when I saw a sign saying "TO THE SALE". I thought it might be interesting, so peddled in the direction in which the sign pointed. It was a house sale. I had never been to one before and I was fascinated. Leaving my bike in a hedge I joined the throng of people in the house and watched while they bid for pictures and furniture, china and glass and all manner of interesting things in the kitchen. Then it was time for the outside goods to be sold. By this time I saw how things were done and when some bundles of raspberry canes came up and no one bid, up shot my hand and in a loud voice cried, "A bob!" There was a ripple of laughter but the auctioneer, a young, fair haired man, kept a straight face and solemnly knocked them down to me. I was enchanted, I had bought something for the back garden, next year we would have our very own raspberries.

I followed the trail of people going into the office and paid my shilling and with the receipt in my hand collected the large bundle, which I had great difficulty balancing on the bike, and had to walk home pushing it, while holding on to my prize.

The first person I met on my return was my father. "Look, Daddy" I cried in delight, "I went to a sale and bought these for a bob, will you put them in the garden for me?"

My father cast a despairing glance to heaven and exploded. "My God, here we are on our beam ends and the child goes off and buys raspberry canes!"

Not long after that the hotel venture came to an end. The furniture was sold, our belongings once again packed up. Daddy went off to Bristol and Mother and I went back to Foxhill. Calmly I accepted another move but it worried me that perhaps the next people would not plant my lovely raspberry canes!

CHAPTER
TEN

A Little Learning

We stayed with my grandparents all that autumn, over Christmas and into the spring. I think it was about April that the fateful message came over the 'phone to say my father had been killed in an accident. Mother was very shocked but soon pulled herself together and set off alone for Bristol.

In those days very little was told to children and I was eleven at the time, so still considered too young to know any facts. I just knew I should not see Daddy any more, which I found hard to believe, but one did not ask about such things of adults.

My mother came back, she wore a black coat and hat for a while and a grey dress with a white collar and I had a black arm band sewn to the sleeve of my overcoat.

By July, Mother had decided it was time for me to go to school again and in the late August we picked up yet another set of door keys and moved to a first floor flat in a house at the head of one of the Thames reaches at Caversham.

I never knew how my mother managed, as in later years I found out that Daddy had only left £2,000 in a family trust for me, and Mother got the interest of £1 a week paid monthly. As she was always "subbing", it was either a feast or a famine.

Anyway she took the flat and bought some furniture on hire-purchase from Bulls the furniture shop in Reading. We had bedding and curtains left over from the hotel. The flat, which consisted of a bedroom, sitting room, bathroom and kitchen, had wooden floors which Mother stained brown and some mats appeared and soon we, Mother, myself and the dogs, were comfortable, and I started my first term at a small girls' school on Caversham Heights. I think the fees were £5 a term and then extras for drawing, singing and elocution. As I had never had much schooling or mixed much with girls of my own age, I found myself at a bit of a loss. Eventually, after the initial awkwardness when I was routinely ignored, the girls started to talk to me. However, I only made one long lasting friend, a girl called Betty Arthur, and we corresponded for many years and once met at a horse show where my small daughter was riding. I think the experience put her off as I never heard from her again!

For the two years I was at Hemdean House I was mainly happy.

This small school had once been a day and boarding establishment, but the old head, Miss Kennet, had just retired and boarding discontinued. The old lady, then white haired and rather bent, came often to the school and was greatly loved by the pupils. The new head, Miss Ada Ida Olivey, was a graduate of Girton, I believe. A tall, black haired woman in her thirties; a great teacher but a stern disciplinarian. She quickly discovered I had a small talent for writing and I was encouraged to produce compositions, although sometimes she would sigh and shake her head and say, "Peggy, I asked for a composition not a book!".

She also started me on Latin which I loved and the two years I was there I learned a little of that wonderful language which has stood me in good stead. I often feel that being able to write well enough to put a little jam on the bread and butter is due in many ways to Miss Olivey's interest and teaching.

Maths still bewildered me, I could do mental arithmetic and that was all. My first lesson in Algebra was my last when I asked the mistress "Why call it x, why not just leave it a?". She said she did not think I had the right attitude and so the head called my mother in and suggested I have further elocution lessons instead at a £1 a term extra, and my mother agreed, although she must have privately wondered where the extra money would come from.

Being a high spirited child and a real tomboy, I was soon in trouble for climbing trees in the school orchard and hanging upside down from the branches.

"Not something we expect young ladies to do!"

I spent a good deal of time in detention after school writing lines or copying large chunks of the King James Bible. The bits that stuck in my mind have come in very useful for crossword solving and quizzes over the years.

The school house keeper, Mrs Orchard, a lovely round lady with snow white hair and a rosy cheeked face, cooked a lunch for those of us who stayed, which

I did on occasions. Mother was very busy doing her paintings which she sold to keep us, book covers, matchbox covers in vellum and tea and coffee trays.

Most days I walked down the hill to home for lunch and once I found Mother red eyed and knew she had been crying. An awful tragedy had occurred. Mother's Yorkies did not usually take much notice of anyone, being devoted to her, but that morning one of them, Molly her favourite, had apparently tried to follow me when I went to school and had been run over and killed just outside the house. We both sat there and could not eat a thing. Molly was a sweet, inoffensive little soul and rarely came to me, so why, on that fateful day, she had tried to follow me remained a mystery.

On my 12th birthday Mother organised a party for me and about eight girls from school were invited. We had a great time and Mother made a lovely tea and for one of the games each girl was given two rolls of crepe paper, scissors and glue and had to construct a fancy dress for herself within twenty minutes. I made myself a crinoline and bonnet and won first prize which, as Mother judged, perhaps was not the most tactful thing to have done, but none of the other girls had managed to make much in the way of a costume.

We stayed at the flat until the next spring and when I came home from school one day it was to find everything packed up. Nothing was said but I think we had not paid the rent. I was not very enamoured with this flat except that it was by the Thames and one of my school friends' family had a boat and twice I joined them for an evening on the river, when we played a gramophone, ate sandwiches, drank lemonade and had a most enjoyable time.

Mother said our furniture would have to go in store and that for a while it was back to furnished rooms again.

Turning yet another key in a front door. It was a semi-detached house in a quiet street in Caversham. We rented two rooms and a slip of a kitchen and shared the bathroom.

The landlord, who occupied most of the house, was an Indian gentleman, very softly spoken and courteous. He had a business colouring all shapes and sizes of vases and used a cellulose spray, the fumes from which perfumed the whole house and the garden, sometimes it was almost stifling. What with that and the strong smell of mother's oil paints, we lived in a pretty toxic atmosphere.

I do not know whether it was this or some other cause, but we had not been there a few weeks when I went down with quinsy. This is nasty illness as one's throat tends to close up.

Our landlord informed mother he was a faith healer and would come up, free of charge, and cure me. He sat on the side of my bed and held my hand and with his eyes closed and his nose pointing at the ceiling he chanted in a low voice. I felt so ill I did not care much. I was no better and it took the local doctor and his potions to effect a cure.

I was off school for most of the term and, when I did return, found out how nasty schoolgirls can be when they said I had not been ill at all but just avoiding school.

Neither Mother nor I could put up with the cellulose smell any longer, so moved up on to Caversham Heights and turned the' key in the door to a house owned by a Mr and Mrs Cummings.

We had a bedroom and sitting room and share of the kitchen and bathroom.

I well remember the landlady's horrified face when she came in and found my mother's trays and paints all spread over the furniture. She was not keen on the dogs either and I guessed we would not be there long.

I was now spending my spare time writing, mostly stories and comic verses. I used to write the notes for the milkman such as

> A pint of milk please milkman dear
> And now to tire your legs,
> I'll ask you just to run outside
> And fetch us six large eggs!

Although unlikely to help me become Poet Laureate, the milkman was so delighted with his verses that he collected them and told my mother his wife had pasted them in a scrap book!

I hated Mrs Cummings' house, it was not like home and she spent her time complaining about the smell of oil paints and the dogs and Mother set about finding us yet another place to live.

Our next landlady could be described as "a character". She was middle height, of advanced years and with wild, grey hair fastened by innumerable hairpins, which she shed about the house. Arrayed in a variety of garments and with several scarves floating about her shoulders, she wore large boots both in and out of doors. For my part I did not mind what she looked like for the house was detached and stood in a big garden with several climbable trees.

We had two large rooms and our own small kitchen and bathroom. Our sitting room had French windows onto the lawn and as it was late spring both the dogs and I were happy.

This resting place was nearer to school, so I could cycle there and back each day and back and forth for lunch.

My elocution lessons with Miss Clutterbuck were bearing fruit and I was entered for the London Royal Academy of Music elocution examinations. For these one had to attend at dusty old St Mary's Hall in The Butts at Reading. I spent a lot of time rehearsing for my exams and Mother must have got heartily sick of my Shakespearian declarations, from "Make me a willow cabin at your gate" to Juliet's impassioned speech "Cut him out in little stars that all the world may be in love with night". This coupled with the ordinary elocution lessons in class which involved learning the whole of "Hiawatha" one term and "The Lay of the Last Minstrel" the next, and as I spent a good deal of time striding round house and garden declaiming my lines my poor mother must has been deeved to death.

I passed all my exams up to Grade Five and this was far more difficult with a long speech by Imogen from Cymberline and then a duet of two voices with her father. There were also parts of the throat to be learned and how the voice was produced. By the time the exam was due I heartily loathed Imogen.

The day of the exam dawned at last and we sat in the waiting room at the dusty hall with countless other girls and their mothers from various schools round Reading, and at last it was my turn to go in.

All the examiners I encountered were elderly men in fusty looking suits peering myopically through thick glasses. I had about half an hour's hard graft that day and came out wet with perspiration. We had to sit and wait until the card bearing our marks was brought out and given to us; on the side of mine something was written. I took one horrified look and cried. "Oh Mummy, it says Disgusting!". It was in fact "Distinction"!

So delighted was Miss Clutterbuck with my success that she insisted I try for the bronze medal two years before I should have done. Alas I failed by three marks to pass, and so ended my examination career. I have, however, had cause to be grateful for those lessons in voice production as I have had to speak quite a lot in public and at least never need to use a microphone, having been taught to reach the listeners at the back of the hall, however large!

We were settled quite happily in our new rooms and Mother was able to get on with her painting, still making coffee trays, book covers and the like for a number of stores. One of these was Marshall and Snelgrove in Oxford Street, and when Mother went up to see the buyer, was told that Queen Mary had been in the shop, which she visited regularly, and seen one of Mother's coffee trays and later one of the ladies in waiting returned and bought it. We were very thrilled and hoped this was the start of prosperity, but nothing more came of it.

One day my mother rescued a young jackdaw that had fluttered down into the garden and was too young and unfledged to fly away. As jackdaws will, he became, in a very short time, a member of the family. He was great fun and soon learned to fly properly but did not go away. He flew in and out of the door to the garden, perched on Mother's shoulder when she was painting and when she came in with a tray of food would fly down and gather a beakful of whatever attracted him and fly off again.

At the time I was absorbing the poems in Ingoldsby's Legends and one, which Mother used to recite when I was much younger, "The Jackdaw of Rheims" was my favourite. I liked to recite this poem, especially to Jack, who would put his head on one side and look quite interested when I declaimed . . .

In and out. Through the motley rout,
That little jackdaw kept hopping about;
Here and there. Like a dog at a fair,
Over comfits and cakes. And dishes and plates,
Cowl and cope and rochet and pall,
Mitre and crosier, he hopped upon all!

Of course he did not get away with just listening to the first verse but had to show interest in the rest of the poem.

The story tells how the Cardinal took off his ring, and the jackdaw, when no one was looking, picked it up and flew away with it, "There was a cry and a shout. And a deuce of a rout . . . ".

Knowing this poem so well I should have twigged when silver spoons started to go missing and the trouble began. The landlady, whose name I have long forgotten, made a great fuss and accused my mother of taking them and mixing them with ours. There was quite a scene. Then Mother's tubes of oil paint also started disappearing and the landlady's silver earrings. A great storm arose. Lastly Mother's wrist watch vanished.

Mother's idea of a sneak thief was discounted and the landlady accused her of stealing her own things to avoid blame!

Things had got to a pretty pass when climbing one of the apple trees by the fence I happened to look down on the roof of the garage in the next door garden, there, in the guttering, were all the stolen goods plus a few more, Jack the Daw had obviously taken the story of "The Jackdaw of Rheims" very much as a pattern for life!

"Why didn't we think of this before?" exclaimed my mother, "especially as we both know the poem so well!".

The landlady was glad to get her things back but resolutely refused to apologise to my mother, who was naturally very hurt and determined that we move from the house. The drama, however, was not ended, for Mother and I were all packed and waiting for transport, with Jack the Daw in a little cage when the landlady stormed in and demanded the bird be left as it was hers. It had landed in her garden, so it was her property. Such a scene, and then the transport came and to avoid a doorstep confrontation, poor Jack had to be handed over, and once again we handed back another set of house keys and moved back to Foxhill and my grandparents.

CHAPTER
ELEVEN

A Pie for Pingey

Our next house was in fact a bungalow at Sonning Common, just outside Reading. At that time the village was in the process of being developed. Buildings were springing up all over the place. Our bungalow was in an unadopted road leading to beautiful woods full of oak and beech and carpeted with primroses and bluebells in spring.

The bungalow was new and raw, it had two bedrooms, a living room, bathroom and kitchen and a sizeable "garden", a long patch of rough uncultivated ground. My mother said the rent was a pound a week. We had a little furniture but no carpets, so once again Mother was on her knees with the floor stain and went right through the rooms.

The kitchen was tiny with a larder on the south side of the house, it got so hot that it was impossible to keep any meat or milk in there without it going bad.

I could get to school by bus and had company, as three of my school fellows came from a family who farmed a large acreage outside the village. The farm had a wonderful cherry orchard and I was often down there climbing the trees among the blossom and that summer I helped with the cherry picking.

Not able to carry on with her painting while we were at Foxhill, Mother had lost all her contacts and a living had to be made somehow so she decided to make and sell cakes. She was an excellent and inventive cook and soon her notice in the local post office brought in the custom.

The first customers passed the good news round and a thriving business was established. After school it was my job to cycle round to the various houses delivering cakes.

One elderly lady I had to visit had a very vicious old mongrel dog called Springtime, whom she referred to as "Pingey". "He won't let you in the gate" she told me, "unless you bring a pie for Pingey". So every time I delivered cakes to the house I had to have a cake or pastry handy to stuff in the old dog's mouth and then he let me through the gate!

Apart from the Yorkshire terriers, of which there were now three, Tweedie, another bitch and a young dog, I had two cats grandly christened Peter Titum and Paulina Teedeedle. They lived with and behaved like the dogs, coming on long walks through the woods and having wonderful games rushing up and down the trees.

Although Tweedie was not a markedly good specimen of her breed, she did have that long and imposing pedigree and Mother had desperately wanted her to have puppies. Tweedie visited several noted studs over a couple of years but nothing happened. Then while at the Common, when she came in season she somehow escaped from the house and returned pursued by around a dozen dogs of assorted sizes and no obvious breed! She also got coupled with mother's young dog and I discovered them outside the backdoor. "What are they doing?" I asked mother in amazement, but answer came there none and I was bundled indoors.

At the appointed time with a nice bed in the sitting room in which to deliver her puppies, Tweedie vanished. We searched high and low and then when I was in the shed feeding my cages of assorted rabbits and guinea pigs I heard a squeak from under the hay piled in the corner.

Right at the back Tweedie had made a snug nest and there she was curled up with six puppies!

The illicit family grew and thrived and all were different, one a blue and tan and looking a bit like a Yorkie but the others black and white, brown and white, all brown and so on! Mother was most ashamed of the motley crew and was quite relieved when they left for new homes. It was Tweedie's only assay into motherhood.

In the summer, there was a grand fete on the common and I won a side of bacon in a bowling competition. In glee we carried it home, as rations were always scarce, and hung it in the larder. Alas, the heat and the invading blue bottles ensured that we did not enjoy very much of this prized delicacy.

Mother was an enthusiastic gardener and with a large uncultivated expanse at her command, decided to make an Italian sunken garden. Anything more impractical in our state of finance could hardly be imagined! However, she engaged an odd job man who dug her a large sunken expanse, but that was as far as it went. Paying him took all the spare cash, there was none left for plants! In time nature took over and the embryo Italian garden was soon overgrown with grass and weeds.

It was at this stage that I became something of a miser, hiding what precious coins I had behind the wallpaper and at one stage putting them in a cocoa tin and burying it in the garden. Here I ran into trouble as I had not marked the spot and after a few months, needing my hoarded pennies, I had to dig up quite a large patch to find it.

If mother's income at that time was derived from home-made cakes and pies, mine was from my prolific family of rabbits and guinea pigs who provided a steady stream of youngsters which found a ready sale.

Possibly because of my actress step-sister, but also because I loved literature of all sorts, especially Shakespeare, the proximity of the theatre at Reading was a temptation.

Reading was noted for its theatre, to which came well-known professional companies. In addition it played host to a very fine amateur dramatic society who put on Shakespeare and light opera as well as serious plays by Russian dramatists.

Most terms we were taken to the theatre by the school, but when I had saved up enough to pay for two seats, Mother and I went together. Mother was never a lover of Shakespeare and endured it for my sake. I could hear her deep sighs during the performance and once or twice she dozed off. It never spoilt my enjoyment.

One touring company was that of Sir Frank Benson, then a very old man and enjoying about his twelfth farewell tour. The school took us to see his "Hamlet" which he played with all the verve of a much younger man. However for myself and my school friends we only had eyes for the handsome young actor playing Laertes. Unknown at that time he rose to fame as Robert Donat.

My visit to this play also sticks in my memory for the fact that I had raging toothache at the time. All through my childhood I had bouts of toothache but was never taken to a dentist. Mother said this was because she had had a bad experience of a dentist when young, but I think it was possibly because we could not afford a visit. The attacks were doctored by the application of Oil of Cloves or whisky rubbed on the gums, none of which had much effect. The abscess just had to go of its own accord.

I was enthralled by Louisa Alcott's "Little Women", and when I heard of a poor family improbably called "Emmett", living in the village, I took it upon myself to befriend them taking food we could not spare and some of my old toys and little trinkets to amuse the children. It was only when I heard they sold both to fund the husband's drinking habit that I realised that doing good works was not all it was cracked up to be!

Looking back, I believe that our stay at Sonning Common was as brief as most of the houses we lived in during my childhood. I suppose once again Mother found it impossible to manage, and then my grandmother sent an urgent SOS. The maids had left, could Mother go back to Foxhill at once?

It was convenient for all parties, and once again we packed up.

CHAPTER
TWELVE

Growing Up

It was no hardship for me to leave Sonning Common as I was to go back to my beloved Foxhill where we stayed on for all that year until I left school at the age of fourteen, with no examinations to my credit. In those days it was Marticulation, which standard we did not reach. At fourteen the girls left Hemdean and went on to one of the big schools in Reading, the Abbey or Kendrick, for higher education.

This was not for me, the fees would have been prohibitive and, anyway, I had had enough of other girls. I loved the lessons though and have so often regretted not having a more formal education. I have just had to read a great deal and pick up what I could from life as it came along.

I left school at the end of the Christmas term after a disastrous experience. Due to take the part of Titania in the fairy scenes from "A Midsummer Night's Dream", I caught a severe chill at the dress rehearsal and ended up in bed with a roaring temperature. All through the two years and a term I had been at Hemdean, I had, as the "star" elocution pupil, had to recite at the end of term concerts "Old Nicholas Nye" (with suitable actions!) and a chunk or two of Shakespeare, and "I remember the house where I was born". All had gone quite well but Titania was going to be my triumph and swan song. Alas, it was not to be, teaching me not to count any chickens before they are hatched!

Why, when Grannie's domestic problems were solved that spring with the engagement of Florence as cook-housekeeper, a position she occupied until my grandmother's demise quite some years later, did Mother rent a small period cottage in a Sussex village? I do not even know how she came to find it as we had no friends in that neighbourhood and she had no work or pressing need to live in the locality. But we went. It was a delightful old cottage. All oak floors and beams and with the proverbial roses growing over the porch. I am not sure quite how we survived, as the only job I had was as cattery maid to a very rich lady in the nearby town. This did not last more than a few months and only brought in ten shillings a week. We heard later that after I left, the lady, a dumpy, middle-aged red-head, ran off with her young and handsome chauffeur. No doubt he had an eye to the main chance, as she was no oil painting! I got some occasional work on a local farm, reared some poultry and sold eggs, and we cultivated the small garden and grew vegetables.

The local store was run by a quiet sect who wore brown habits, they were called Coaklers, the locals calling them Coakleys. We never really knew their correct name. They kept themselves to themselves and apart from seeing them in the shop they were never seen around the village. On Sundays their melodious singing wafted from the small chapel that backed onto the stream that bordered our garden. They made and baked the most delicious bread. Much of our diet consisted of their loaves as they were comparatively cheap.

My step-sister came to stay between engagements and was charmed by the cottage and its location. She brought her latest rescue with her, a black, white and tan mongrel terrier with a rough coat and a tail that curled over his back, his name was Whoopee. It was at the time when hysteria was rife in dogs and Whoopee was a martyr to it. Suddenly he would start howling and flying round the little sitting room, banging into furniture and once ran right up the wall! It was found later that the dog biscuits being manufactured contain an ingredient called "agene" which caused hysteria. Once the manufacturers realised this and left out the rogue ingredient, things went back to normal. Mother's Yorkies did not have that sort of biscuit so we had no trouble with them. Barbara managed to keep Whoopee with her for some years, at least she never asked Mother to take him on.

One evening when we had gone upstairs, Barbara came into Mother's room and perched on the side of the bed. With a loud crack, one of the legs went clean through the ceiling beneath. We were laughing so much we did not realise the floor was rotten with woodworm and it was only by good luck that the whole did not give way and catapult us into the sitting room. Mother pooh-poohed the fact that the floor might collapse and next day just nailed a piece of wood over the hole and we hoped for the best.

It was at this point that my mother became embroiled with some local ladies who were organising a pageant. I am not sure if they were celebrating some local event, but as it involved Saint Augustine I do not think so. Mother took on the role of producer and very good she was too. Her small amount of theatrical experience and her flair for organisation and with a good ear for the spoken word ensuring that she soon had the cast rehearsing in a very professional manner. The lady who ran the whole show was the President of the local branch of the Women's Institute and lived in a large house with much land. She also had a very good-looking son called Christian who was at Oxford, and came down during rehearsals. I thought he was something special but a long-haired, gangling, gauche, fifteen year old did not interest him. No wonder!

It was decided that the pageant needed a prologue to set the scene, but in the script there was no prologue, so Mother said that I had better write one. The lady president was a bit sceptical, but what I produced quite surprised her, I was told.

Bodies being in quite short supply, it was not a cast of thousands but large enough to have taken up all the press-ganged volunteers in the village. I was drafted into the cast as Prologue, draped in a sheet and crown of laurel leaves, and had to declaim my deathless prose from the stage of the village hall.

The pageant was a huge success. So much so that Mother was asked to take on the production of the village pantomime, "The Queen of Hearts". All went well until one of the village families took umbrage at a careless remark and we lost half the chorus in one fell swoop. However, Mother soon dragooned six more village ladies into taking part. There were some good amateurs in the cast, especially the man playing the Yellow Dwarf, who gave a most professional performance.

Mrs R, who insisted on playing the Principle Boy (much against Mother's wishes, as the lady was well past the age to assume such a role) was, however, a close friend of the WI president and always given a leading part in whatever was going on in the village. There was, therfore, no argument that could be satisfactorily used to keep her from having the part. She had a lavish set of costumes made by a professional, used a little too much make up and had a rather peculiar singing voice that caused not a few giggles both from the rest of the cast and the audience, who knew her well from other village activities. The Principle Girl was very pretty and had a sweet singing voice. We all felt for her in the duets with her suitor who had a poor idea of sharing a duet and was inclined to bellow. As we were again a bit short of performers, I had to double the parts of Fairy Queen, who only appeared in Act One, and the Knave of Hearts, a far better part. I enjoyed swaggering on and off in tights and tabard! It was a good job I did not have a number to sing. Mr Carol, the singing master at school (yes, truly that was his name), used to make me sit on one side during singing lessons and keep my mouth shut as he said if I started singing I put everyone else out of tune as well!

We took the pantomime to several other villages and received good notices in the local press. After Christmas they asked Mother to produce a variety programme and I dared a song and dance routine. It must have been awful, but the audience did clap quite dutifully. We had a local man who played and sang to his guitar, who was the star. I thought him wonderful and used to stand on the side of the stage and listen to every song. By then Christian had gone back to Oxford. However, my latest object of admiration was in his thirties and happily married!

It was just about this time that I at last succeeded in persuading my mother to allow me to have my long hair cut off. What a joy it was to see all those inhibiting and embarrassing tresses lying on the hairdresser's floor. Mother had decided I should have my hair permed and spent some time saving the £5 (the cost at the time), an astronomical sum in our lives.

At that time, the whole process took hours and I remember being strung up to a machine that was several feet from the floor. The perm was a Eugene. It lasted about three weeks and then dropped out, the result was less than attractive and at fifteen one takes such things a bit to heart! Each night I rolled my short hair up in curlers, which were very uncomfortable to sleep on. When we were going out anywhere my mother used to put a curl or wave in my poker-straight locks with her curling tongs, which were brought to the correct temperature over a little heater which ran on methylated spirit.

One of my mother's acquaintances from the amateur dramatic scene introduced us to her son, a good-looking young man of about eighteen. He had been at public school when he contracted polio, fortunately in a mild form, but it left him very lame. I thought he was madly romantic with his dark hair flopping over his forehead, his shadowed eyes and his pronounced limp. He came to tea several times and once we went to pick primroses in the nearby wood.

Alas, nothing came of that either!

Tall evening primroses grew by the gate and the low stone wall was a mass of nasturtiums of all different colours. The smell of either flower can transport me back to that Sussex cottage and remind me of how embarrassing growing up could be!

I am not sure how we managed to survive in this cottage but it all came to one of those sudden ends triggered when a local fox killed all my chicken.

Mother had been longing to live in London again, although she had not done so for many years, and one day caught a train to the Big Smoke and when she came back said she had rented a flat in Upper Norwood not far from Crystal Palace.

So various things were sold, the rest packed up ready for the removal van, and once again we moved to a new dwelling.

My childhood was behind me and I suppose I thought everything would be different, but it was not, we went on moving house, and I can truthfully say that

I can pack up and move house in 24 hours and know exactly what is in every box, a skill learned when young from my mother! This stood me in good stead as I married a man, also with itchy feet, and I have been called on to put my expertise in house moving to good use on a large number of occasions. I can even motivate removal men and that is not something everyone can boast about! A friend once told me that she kept three pages free in her address book to record our various changes of dwellings.

The cottage I live in now has been home for 12 years, the longest I have ever lived in one place, which was why Foxhill in my childhood was so precious, it was always there to go back to when the going got too rough. But would I have been any happier just to live in one place? A moot point. Variety, they say, is the spice of life and travel broadens the mind and all the other old clichés.

The ability to cope was undoubtedly taught me by my mother who was the most capable person able to turn her hand to anything as the situation demanded and unflappable in any crisis no matter how grim. The expression, a stiff upper lip, must have been coined by someone who knew her! As a consequence I am impatient with women who complain of stress, cannot manage their children or animals, cook a decent meal or deal successfully with an awkward husband!

From my father I learned that life was to be enjoyed, that a smile and a laugh could indeed turn away wrath and a ready tongue and quick wit is helpful in any situation.

A childhood such as mine does prepare you for all sorts of eventualities and as long as you can keep a sense of humour all will be well. Flexibility is the name of the game. Take what life throws at you and throw it right back. If nothing is happening then go out and make something happen.

To me life has been either a feast or a famine, you have to take both as they come, treat one with caution, the other with respect and do not make a drama out of a crisis!

ISIS publish a wide range of books in large print, from fiction to biography. Any suggestions for books you would like to see in large print or audio are always welcome. Please send to the Editorial department at:

ISIS Publishing Ltd.
7 Centremead
Osney Mead
Oxford OX2 0ES
(01865) 250 333

A full list of titles is available free of charge from:
Ulverscroft large print books

(UK)
The Green
Bradgate Road, Anstey
Leicester LE7 7FU
Tel: (0116) 236 4325

(Australia)
P.O Box 953
Crows Nest
NSW 1585
Tel: (02) 9436 2622

(USA)
1881 Ridge Road
P.O Box 1230, West Seneca,
N.Y. 14224-1230
Tel: (716) 674 4270

(Canada)
P.O Box 80038
Burlington
Ontario L7L 6B1
Tel: (905) 637 8734

(New Zealand)
P.O Box 456
Feilding
Tel: (06) 323 6828

Details of **ISIS** complete and unabridged audio books are also available from these offices. Alternatively, contact your local library for details of their collection of **ISIS** large print and unabridged audio books.